T0129731

*f*P

TOMMY & Me

THE MAKING OF A DAD

BEN STEIN

THE FREE PRESS
New York London Toronto Sydney Singapore

THE FREE PRESS
A Division of Simon & Schuster Inc.
1230 Avenue of the Americas
New York, NY 10020

Designed by Kim Llewellyn

Manufactured in the United States of America
10 9 8 7 6 5 4 3 2 1

Library of Congress Cataloging-in-Publication Data
Stein, Benjamin, 1944–
Tommy and me : the making of a dad / Ben Stein
p. cm.
ISBN 0-684-83896-6
1. Fatherhood. 2. Fathers and sons. 3. Adopted children.
I. Title.
HQ756.S76 1998
306.874'2—dc21 98-12121
CIP

ISBN 978-1-9821-3498-3

For Peter Feierabend

CONTENTS

PREFACE
The Glory of Love

On about January 4, 1998, I was up in Northern Idaho, a place you will hear more about, snowshoeing and watching my ten-year-old son Tommy and his friends snowboard. After a tiring day in the cold, Tommy and his best friend, Alexander, came back to our little motel on the lake (forty-eight dollars per night per room, one room for us and one for his friend and for playing video games). The boys played video games and watched movies. I sat at my laptop and wrote. After we had pizza sent in at about nine, I told my son he could stay up until twelve but not a moment later.

At about ten, I spoke to a friend in Los Angeles who had just returned from a trip to St. Barts in the Caribbean, where he had cruised on another friend's hundred-and-fifty-foot yacht. "The amazing thing is," my friend told me breathlessly, "that there are hundreds of yachts like this. And a lot of people we know had yachts that were two hundred feet or two hundred and fifty feet. Ron Perelman, the guy who owns Revlon, had two two-hundred-foot yachts, one for parties and one for sailing. Ted Field had a yacht. Puff Daddy had a yacht.

Each one more lavish than the next. I feel like the loser of the universe. I don't have a plane or a yacht and all of these people have both. What an experience."

I hung up the phone and looked in on my son and his friend playing some scary game. It was eleven-forty-five. "It's time to get ready for bed," I told my son.

Tommy marched over to me and looked up at me with his perfect face. "But, Daddy," he said, "you said we could stay up until twelve."

"All right, my boy, then stay up until twelve. But then it's right to bed."

"Okay, Daddy," Tommy said and went back to his endgame of blood and guts on the video screen.

Suddenly I was overcome with gratitude and joy. Tears came to my eyes. I got down on my knees and prayed with thanks to God that Tommy so completely accepted my being his Daddy, that he was so happy, that he just called me "Daddy" as naturally as if he said "cat" or "dog," and just assumed that I would make the rules and we would both live by them once Daddy had said them.

As I prayed, Tommy came back into the room and saw me on the floor. "What are you doing, Daddy?" he asked.

I looked at him and said, "Well, to tell you the truth, I'm praying. Right now, I'm praying with thanks for you, my boy."

Tommy did not say anything, but he stood next to me and smiled and then went back to his game. That night, as he lay in the bed next to mine, he read his ghastly science fiction for a while and said, "I am not going to sleep until you go to sleep and then you have to tell me a story about who invented tanks."

In the night, snow fell in North Idaho. By the time Tommy and I got up, it was falling in buckets, covering the lawn that runs from the motel to the marina and the immense frozen lake. Tommy and his friend Alexander ate breakfast and then ran out into the snow. It was traveling day, and I faced the awesome task of packing Tommy's mass of mess into his bags and also packing my own. I slid open the windows to the lawn. Tommy and Alex were building a snow fort, burying each other in snow, and trying to rub snow in each other's faces.

"Daddy," Tommy said. "Come play with us in the snow."

"I can't, my boy. I have to pack our bags."

"Come on, Daddy," he pleaded. "How often can we play in the snow?"

He was right, of course. I went down and helped to bury Alexander in the snow, and then I tossed snowballs (very softly) at Tommy. Then I refereed a snow fight between Tommy and Alex, and finally, helped to shake the snow out of Tommy's perfect flaxen hair. How many times, indeed, will I get to do that?

After he came back to the room and sat panting on the edge of the bed, I stared at him. He looked flushed, excited, ecstatic. His skin was bright red and his eyes glowed blue gray. I hope Ron Perelman and Ted Field and the other hundreds in St. Barts with their yachts are one hundredth as happy with their boats and their millions as I was with my little boy in our motel room. I hope their lives have as much meaning—getting to be even more rich and to have even more status—as mine did helping Tommy to pack his pal Alexander in snow.

Moments like that are what this book is about: how working and playing at the world's best job, Tommy's Dad, has given my life meaning beyond what I had dreamed possible. It's also about how that meaning has given me moments of satisfaction far, far beyond what I would have thought possible.

It didn't happen overnight or smoothly. That's what this book is about, too: how I got from nowhere, Daddy-wise, to a lovely, although adventurous, patch of life.

I thought of calling this book *Fatherhood and Meaning,* but that is too portentous for a book about having a good time. Yet it's also what the book is about: Once I stopped resisting the responsibility of fatherhood, once I got my priorities straight about fatherhood as compared with everything else, my life was far easier, calmer, and better, not harder or more painful. It's a lot better at three in the afternoon and incomparably better at three in the morning.

The plan of the book is as follows: Mostly it goes in straight chronological order. But alternating with each straight chronological chapter is a "bookmark" as I coyly call it. This is about an incident out of chronology that says how life is now or was very recently with my perfect little angel. The parts out of chronological order are simply noted with italics. At the end of the book are what I have found to be ten excellent rules about fatherhood. There are obviously many more such rules, just as in the Hebrew religion there are far more *mitzvot* than the Ten Commandments, but ten is a readily usable number, easy to work with and clean. I have referred to fathers and sons, but I believe the rules also apply to fathers and daughters.

In writing this book, I have to acknowledge first my wife, a true saint, a living breathing goddess of goodness, intelligence, and good sense, not to mention wit and beauty. Then David Radis and Pam Morton, without whose help there would be no book, deserve lavish praise. I also thank Dr. James Dobson, a truly brilliant man I have never met, and another braino, Paul Hyman, a genius of family relationships. I truly thank deeply the members of the Spiritual Search group during my stay at the Malibu Community Center, noon meeting, especially from 1988 to 1992. You guys saved my life. I thank my parents and my wife's parents, my sister, and Michael Chinich, who gave some very valuable advice at a crucial time. I also thank Adam Bellow, who bought this book and encouraged me endlessly, and Liz Maguire and Chad Conway, who stayed on the job when Adam left to write his own book. The kind editors of *The American Spectator, Washingtonian, The American Enterprise,* and *Reader's Digest* have published my thoughts on Tommy for years. I thank them.

I was blessed beyond measure to have Peter Feierabend in my life, if only briefly. I think of him every day, always with tears. Most of all, I thank the Almighty God, who gave me, a most undeserving mortal, the chance to serve as father to Tommy Stein. It is my main task and pleasure every day to deserve this child.

TOMMY & Me

INTRODUCTION

Let's start in midair. On Tuesday, July 23, 1996, my eight-year-old son, Tommy, and I boarded Alaska Airlines Flight 557, scheduled to fly from Los Angeles to Spokane, Washington, via Seattle. We had been up at our rented lakeside home in Sandpoint, Idaho, for a week before that, boating and biking. But we had returned to Los Angeles for the weekend to see my beautiful lawyer wife, Tommy's mother, who was stuck in L.A. on a legal matter.

Now we were on our way back to Idaho. Spokane is about a two-hour drive from Sandpoint and is the closest airport to that lovely town. We were sitting next to each other, of course, window and aisle, with me reading my *Wall Street Journal,* as usual, and Tommy reading a pebble from his mountain of Garfield comic books, also as usual. Across the aisle was a dead-heading Alaska Airlines pilot, reading a catalogue.

"Daddy," Tommy asked me out of the blue, "what's the fastest plane Alaska flies?"

"I have no idea," I said. "Probably one like this one, an MD-80."

"What's the slowest plane Alaska flies?" Tommy asked me.

"Probably a Dash Eight," I said, "like the little propeller planes we used to fly between Portland and Spokane." But Tommy had returned to his comic book and was back in the world of Garfield and John.

The dead-heading pilot heard this byplay, leaned over, and said, "A plane like this one, an updated MD-80, can do about six hundred miles per hour. That's fast. But they're a bit temperamental." I was about to pass on this intelligence to Tommy, but at just that moment there was a boom and then a huge lurch in the left forward portion of the plane, just under us. The plane spiked sharply to port (that's left, as I have learned), then righted itself and went on. It felt like a small bomb had gone off (this was a few days after the explosion of TWA 800).

Our fellow passengers started to cry and mutter. The pilot came on the PA system and told us, "I'm sure you all just felt that. We can't see anything at all wrong on our gauges but that definitely was not normal so we're going to make an emergency landing at Oakland. Fasten your seat belts and stay in your seats." Behind us we could hear murmurs of terror from our fellow passengers and a symphony of ringing call buttons for the flight attendants, who scurried up and down the aisles grim-faced. I wondered if the pilots had checked the "bomb gauge."

Meanwhile, a certain little eight-year-old had not even taken his head out of the Garfield book during the lurch. He was serene until the announcement, but now he looked worried. He wanted to know why we were landing. "There's some kind of problem," I said. "Maybe a hydraulic something."

"How do hydraulic brakes work?" Tommy asked. Asking questions that require complicated answers and some measure of thought (and therefore distraction from the moment) is one of his ways of dealing with stressful situations. I recall reading that Samuel Johnson did the same thing, only with numbers. (What can I say? I'm his father.)

I explained hydraulic brakes to Tommy, in an approximate way, and I told him about how fast an MD-80 is. I skipped the "temperamental" part. In a few minutes we were on the ground. As we rolled down the runway, three people behind me started to clap and shouted, "We're alive! We're alive!"

An hour later, after a huge struggle with Alaska Airlines to get us on flights that would take us to Spokane and let us sit together, Tommy and I found ourselves sitting next to each other on a row of plastic seats facing the Oakland International Airport runway, where a swarm of mechanics inspected our erstwhile plane. I was trying to sleep. Tommy was eating a slice of pizza. A man awakened me to tell me he was a fan of my character acting from long ago. He apologized for being so effusive and walked away. "He should apologize for waking you up," Tommy said. Then he got out of his chair and squirmed into my arms and sat on my lap.

Tommy was at that time a muscular, thin eight-year-old. Normally, I could not get him to sit on my lap for love, money, or new video games—my standard means of bribery, a big subject in and of itself—but these were special, emergency-landing circumstances. Tommy leaned his head back against my shoulder and brushed my chin with his heavenly, sunny-smelling hair. "Daddy, were you scared?" he asked.

"I was very scared."

"What were you most scared of?" he asked me.

"I was most scared that something would happen and I wouldn't get to have you sit on my lap ever again," I said.

Tommy is not a sentimental kid, at least not outwardly, but he kept his head on my shoulder just a second longer than normal before he got up and said, "I want another piece of pizza," and that second, as all father–child conspiracy theorists know, made all the difference. It meant that when he realized the problem, he had been scared of something like what I had been afraid of.

"You were very brave, my boy," I said to him. "I think when we get back to Sandpoint, I'll buy you a mountain bike just to use in Idaho, as a reward for your bravery. And as a memento of this very scary day."

"Can it be a titanium model with handmade shocks?" he asked, referring to one he had seen at a pro mountain biker shop the week before. (Bribery has its downside.)

"No, it cannot. It can be a little boy's model, and I think you're pretty lucky that I'm getting it for you."

"I think we're pretty lucky that we're here on the ground right now," Tommy said. "Thank you, Daddy, for my new mountain bike. Can we go get it tomorrow?"

"If we're not too exhausted from this trip," I said.

As Tommy trotted off with his peculiar skipping/running gait to get his second slice of pizza, I remembered another incident in midair, in 1987, that had something to do with Tommy: In late October of that year, *GQ* magazine ran a humor story by yours truly about some jokes Joan Rivers had made at the memorial service for her recently departed husband, Edgar. Ms. Rivers, possibly genuinely shaken, possibly alert to possibilities for publicity (probably both), took offense at the article and sued me and *GQ* for libel. I hired as my lawyer a very smart fellow I had gone to law school with named John Keker. His office was in San Francisco, so I arranged to fly up there on a 4:30 P.M. flight about two days after the lawsuit was filed. Only about eight weeks before, my wife and I had adopted Tommy at birth, and he was at home with his mom and the nurse while reporters huddled outside my door, trying to get some newsworthy piece of Hollywood gossip out of my plight. Because freeway traffic was unnaturally light on the day of my flight, I got to LAX about an hour early. I was able to get on an earlier shuttle than the one I was scheduled on, and off I went. While I was meeting with Keker, I learned that there had been a disaster. The 4:30 PSA flight, the one I had my ticket on, had crashed. Everyone on board had died. If traffic had been merely normal, not necessarily heavy, I would have been on the flight that crashed. (It crashed, horribly enough, because a disgruntled, recently fired PSA employee had brought a gun aboard and had shot everyone in the cockpit.)

I pray a lot, and I have prayed with thanks over that miracle many times. Now, in that plastic chair in Oakland airport, I prayed with thanks that I had been spared again and was able to go on with my life and, most of all, to have Tommy sit in my lap again. Of all that life means to me, Tommy is the most shining and meaningful part. I had no idea of it at that moment in 1987, but in fact Tommy has become my life since I was allowed to live on that day in late 1987. In a way, it started with some bicyclists and some thieves and with that selfsame John Keker, a great guy, even if he is a Democrat.

ONE

My wife and I are children of the sixties. When we got married back in June of 1968, we had absolutely no plans to have children anytime soon, or ever. Life, as we saw it, was meant to be lived and enjoyed by us. As far as we could tell, the responsibility of children was a stone solid drag and not an enjoyment at all.

We had friends at Yale Law School (where I was a student when my wife, Alexandra, and I were first married) who had children. They looked to be overwhelmed. Their houses or apartments were always a mess, with a slightly ripe odor coming from the bathrooms. They always had to leave parties early—if they were even able to show up. They could not blithely go off to demonstrate against militarism and racism in Washington, or even on the New Haven Green, the way we childless folks could. They could not stay up late getting high on Dewar's Scotch while playing bridge without having to worry about early morning or midnight feedings. Small children cried a lot when you walked them on Elm Street by the law school. How cool could you possibly look with a crying baby on your arm at an emergency meeting of the Ad Hoc

Committee To End The War? How could you possibly be a revolutionary law student if you were at ShopKo buying Pampers?

It's all very well to be a Mexican peasant woman following Zapata with a baby on your hip. But at Yale in the late 1960s, *we* were the babies. We were the demonstrating, shouting, war- and racism-ending babies, and babies do not need or want babies of their own slowing them down.

Plus, both my wife and I had gotten the message from our parents that work and career and success were what counted. At least we thought that was the message we got. Certainly, both of our parental units were ambitious about their careers—and ours—and talked very little, if at all, about the joys of being parents. In fact, up until the time Alexandra and I got married, in 1968, and well beyond, I can't recall my parents ever talking about the exaltation of being parents. In their general demeanor, it was hard to detect much exhilaration about being Mom and Dad. Although this changed a great deal in their later lives, my parents simply never seemed to me to endorse the idea of having children at all or to think it was an important life goal. Instead, my parents seemed to have a constant feeling of shame and anxiety about my behavior, and I thought I detected a wistful, resigned feeling in my mother that what might have been a brilliant career for her as an economist had been short-circuited by her having children. Again, this changed when my parents became elderly, but I really cannot find in my memory any affirmative statement by my parents about parenting until I was at least in my mid-forties.

A painful and revealing moment: After I graduated from Yale Law School as valedictorian of the class of 1970, my mother apologized to Dean Pollak for any criticism of the school in my valedictory address. "He likes to make trouble" is how she put it. What was revealed was a constant burden of having to explain away her errant child, who had just embarrassed her by being valedictorian of his class at Yale. This, at any rate, was what seemed to me to be revealed at that time. As time passes, much of what seemed clear often becomes occluded and vice versa. I had never been a parent, so I had no idea that just being there year after year is how parents express their enthusiasm about being parents. I thought they were supposed to Demonstrate Resolutely for Parent–Child Solidarity and, of course, to Demonstrate for the Moral Superiority of the Child as the Vanguard of the Revolutionary Proletariat.

When Alex and I got out of Yale (law school for me, college for her), it was time for her to go to law school at George Washington University in Washington, D.C., and time for me to practice poverty law and teach about film and revolution at American University. In other words, it was time for us to live our beautiful lives and begin our gilded careers.

In fact, it was also time for us to "have our own space"—an equally trendy and self-defeating, dead-end concept—as well, and we got separated in 1972, with a view toward getting divorced, which we did in 1974. In that time, I was a trial lawyer, a lawyer dropout/hippie type in glorious Santa Cruz, California, and then a speech writer for Richard M. Nixon. I walked through redwood forests and breathed in star jasmine.

What seemed to me and to my circle of peers to be time-optimizing and life-optimizing behavior was this: get high, get laid, shoulder the minimum amount of responsibility possible, cop the biggest possible attitude about it, prolong your own childhood indefinitely. These were the desiderata of my peers and me. This was the anthem of our geh-geh generation, as The Who might have put it. Having and caring for children had nothing to do with any part of it. I defy any historian of the era to find a single rock song saying, "Oh, baby, let's smoke some weed, party down, then stop all of that, become responsible citizens, have kids, and then get steady jobs and provide a stable home for the little ones and sacrifice our time and moments of being stoned for them."

This was not only the message of the culture. It was a personal message of the time. Having children was never something suggested by even one girlfriend of the many I had going through my life at that time. Getting pregnant was like getting a tumor. You just had "it" cut out of you. We had our lives to think of. (When I think of the horror of what that actually meant in terms of murder, my blood runs cold and I feel deeply ashamed.)

But life is personal as well as cultural and social. I am not just the end product of the mass culture and the ethos of the day. I, as a person, made a big mistake. As a person, I made bad choices. There were others smarter than I was—John Keker again stands out—who did make better decisions, did have kids earlier, did settle down and act responsibly. Your servant was not just affected by the culture. I was actuated by a highly personal fear that I lacked the ability to be a good parent, that I lacked the strength of character and manly virtues to be a good father. This, too, had much to do with my not having kids. So did plain old laziness. Kids looked like a lot of work (I had no idea how much). Much easier to stay childless by choice and hang with pals than to change diapers and wake up at night for feedings. As I say, I made some extremely poor decisions.

In time, I left Santa Cruz, returned to Washington, D.C., and then moved to New York to be a writer for *The Wall Street Journal*. Then in 1977, I moved to Los Angeles to write books and screenplays and teach law, and to live it up with starlets. But something had changed in swinging America since my wife and I met in 1966 and since the night-blooming jasmine days at Santa Cruz. The man–woman relationship scene was a disaster of anger, fear, and vengefulness. The days of flower power and happy, unguarded love were long gone. Men and women regarded each other now as members of hostile gangs in barely neutral territory, always prepared for a scrap that might leave either or both dead or wounded.

Being single was to be a soldier in nonstop guerrilla combat. The sexual revolution had produced millions of civil wars, with the reds and the whites fighting each other over every phone line, in every restaurant, at every party, in every bed. Whatever modicum of civility had once existed in male–female relationships—at least among singles—was only a dim memory, like the good manners of pre–World War I Vienna. The dating scene in Los Angeles, while productive of good material for stories, was profoundly unsatisfying and even frightening. Night after night I would be out with women whose rage and ignorance were genuinely horrible. (I often think of the blind date I had who on hearing me say that I had recently been a speech writer for Nixon and a columnist for *The Wall Street Journal* turned to a friend and said, "Oh, right. Another shoe salesman making up big stories."

Plus, Alex and I missed each other. We had always shared a unique view of the world. We laughed at the same things and the same people, which is a big part of a relationship. We had our imaginary, legendarily powerful and well-connected "Granddad," patterned after our friend David Eisenhower's granddad. We lived for dogs. We cried at *Gone With The Wind* and made dog ears at each other. "Mated for life" sums it up in a way, despite our bizarre history.

In 1977 Alex and I remarried, and she moved into my little hillside home in Hollywood. Life was still mainly about ourselves and getting ahead in our glorious careers, though. I wanted to make it as a writer of books and screenplays and was writing like a madman. Hooked up to my powerful agent, the soon-to-be-legendary Michael Ovitz, I went into nirvana when I sold a script—and then into humiliation and despair when it was dropped (or "put into turnaround," as the studio expression goes). My life consisted of feeling as if I were the Messiah when I had deals and feeling as if I were a leper, as I sat and smoked cigarettes in the dark, when deals fell through. I was making a good living by my modest bureaucrat's standards, but I felt as if my blood were running backwards in my veins when I had a meeting with a studio "executive" to get "notes" on rewriting my scripts.

My print career went better, with a few moderately successful books, both fiction and nonfiction, and a veritable blizzard of articles. I had a staggering volume of magazine articles in the journalistic bloodstream and a syndicated column in about fifty newspapers. My wife was practicing law. We were okay, although not highly successful at all by "Hollywood standards" (which exist to make 99 percent of the people here feel miserable).

In our little family there was still no thought of children. Only one close friend in Hollywood, a successful producer, had children. He and his wife had a son who had developed deafness. This, or so Alex and I thought, was a definite warning about what happens when you let children interrupt your career. As far as we could tell, life was about having money for houses in Aspen (we had one), condos in Palm Springs (ditto), Mercedes convertibles (ditto), first-class travel, and meals anywhere we pleased.

Now, it would be easy, but it would be wrong, to say that my life was empty at that point. It wasn't empty. It was full of junk possessions, junk ambitions, junk self-esteem, and junk ideas about life. It was full of very foolish notions and the material proceeds of those notions. My life was also breathtakingly selfish. It was about *my* income, *my* fame, *my* "creative expression." It was a junky, stupid, selfish way to live.

By making career my god, I had contrived it so that my happiness and peace of mind were totally under the control of men and women who probably did not even remember my name from one meeting to the next. Studio officials, agents, producers—those whose business it was to get control over the brains and spirits of ambitious people and then twist those brains and spirits inside out—had me as their captive and plaything. Turning my guts and my peace of mind over to them was like turning over a breakfast of my liver to a hungry coyote.

Small wonder that my wife and I fought a great deal, vacationed rarely (even with our abundance of houses), and lived in a swamp of envy of those more successful than we were. Hollywood runs on envy and fear, and we were running hard.

The breakthrough idea that maybe we might have children and have our lives mean something came about largely because of a phone call from John Keker, my classmate and lawyer pal, in early 1984. His son, Adam, a high school sophomore or junior, was interested in Hollywood and wanted to spend a month or two there. Could we help? He already had some kind of internship at Paramount through another connection. He needed a place to stay and friends to watch over him. Keker assured us that Adam was a good boy and would be no trouble. We had never been hosts of a teenage boy. But Keker was our pal, so we agreed to do it.

The summer with Adam Keker was a stunning eye-opener. He was interesting, a fine conversationalist, and very well behaved; he had perfect home manners in terms of helping out, never caused us a moment's trouble, and made us think, *If a kid could be as good as this, as much fun to be around, why didn't we have one?* We had the most interesting dinnertime conversations of our lives with this fourteen-year-old. We talked with Adam about how they made the special effects in *Blade Runner* and other great movies, how come *Citizen Kane* lasted and *All the King's Men* didn't, and what you had to do to make it in Hollywood. Our eyes were starting to open, but it was a slow process.

Alex and I talked about having children but then backslid by telling ourselves that this, after all, was John Keker's kid. Keker was a decorated Marine combat hero, a famous trial lawyer, and a stern disciplinarian. We—weak, pitiful, disorganized, and obsessed with our work as we were—could never have kids like Keker's. (I still marvel at the discipline that John instilled in that cheerful boy.)

Then my father began to have heart trouble. He had suffered from heart problems before, but they now seemed to be recurring and very serious. When I went to see him, he seemed deeply happy to see me. I got into the habit of visiting him and my mother frequently in D.C. They brightened so much when I saw them and were so sad when I left that I wondered if I had been mistaken in thinking they had always told me that children were a burden. I can recall very well phoning my father to ask him to do some statistical operation for a book I was writing in the mid-1980s. I had said, "I don't mean to interrupt your day," or something equally silly. My father replied, "What on earth can you imagine I would rather do than help my son?"

The remark moved me deeply—and still does.

Then there were the bicyclists. One Sunday afternoon I was, as usual, sitting in my office typing some damned thing.

Through the fence in the backyard, I saw a group of boys and girls madly bicycling up and down a slight grade, laughing and shouting. I was almost forty, and I recall going to Alex, who was reading a book about famous ballerinas of the twentieth century. "This is so sad," I told her. "We're never going to have children laughing and playing like that on their bikes."

"Well," she said, "maybe we should try."

"But what if it's a disaster? What if they turn out to be maniacs?"

"That's a possibility," she said. "But you aren't that much of a maniac, at least not all of the time."

"And you're not a maniac at all," I added on her behalf. "But how much do children really mean in a life?" I asked.

My wife hit that one right out of the field when she said, "Well, how much do you mean to your parents?" Twenty years before I might have raised my eyebrows at that question, but as Alex asked it I realized the answer was a large quantum indeed.

The final note came at a family-style restaurant called Bob's Big Boy in Burbank. Alex and I had gone there to have a triple-decker. Across from us was a large ethnic family of parents, grandparents, and kids. "We're never going to have kids and grandchildren," I said. "That makes me feel really lonely."

"I guess it's up to us," Alex said.

We decided that we wanted to have children.

By then it was 1984. For over two years, we tried heroically, in the usual fashion, to make a baby. That didn't work. We tried fertility treatments for my bride. She bravely went off to get injections of something called Pergonal, as well as other drugs. She got artificial insemination. She got *in vitro*. Nothing worked.

We started with the then-fashionable route of surrogate mothers. It was a bizarre idea, seemingly handled by bizarre men and women. One man, a lawyer who was supposedly a pioneer in the field of surrogate law, turned out to be questionable indeed. He took five thousand dollars for a consultation and then demanded another five thousand to—as he charmingly put it—"make sure the baby's white." (In L.A., any urgent personal need always brings forth a host of con men.) A woman "psychologist" who supposedly worked in the field was an unbelievable crank. Not only did she take telephone calls while we were in very expensive meetings with her, but she actually *made* totally unrelated phone calls while we were pouring out our hearts to her.

The most stunning thief was a woman lawyer in Santa Monica. We went for a consultation with her. She asked us to sign a paper saying that we understood the legal problems inherent in surrogacy. Then she said that if we proceeded, she wanted a ten-thousand-dollar retainer against four hundred dollars per hour. We said that was excessive and that we would not go further and left. She then sent us a bill for ten thousand dollars. We called to remind her that we had declined her services and had left after only a few minutes. She sent us the retainer document with the signature page from a totally different document (the letter acknowledging the legal problems in surrogacy) affixed to it!

At this discouraging juncture, enter an Angel of Mercy named Pam Morton, who manages my favorite restaurant—Morton's.

It's summer. Monday, at our little rented house on a huge lake in North Idaho. My eight-year-old son, Tommy, and I are watching the sky cloud over after the weekend's stupendous heat.

"Can we go on our boat over to Bottle Bay for lunch?" Tommy asks, just as the raindrops start to fall.

"No. It's dangerous to go on the lake when it's raining. That's basic."

"Can we ride our bikes into town?"

"Sure."

We just got these bikes a few days ago. Tommy's is a powerful new mountain bike. Mine is a used model that some lumber worker down on his luck had to sell. Still, we're roaring along Lake Street, Third Street, Huron, Superior, and then across Route 95 just ahead of a cattle truck coming down from Canada as the rain stops.

"Can we stop and fish?" Tommy asks.

"Sure."

We stop at the boat and get out Tommy's fishing gear. Then he fishes under the deck of a lakeside restaurant while I wrestle with our boat's cover, which never seems to fit right. "Daddy," he says every time there's a bite. "Daddy."

"Did you catch something?"

"I caught two little ones," he says. "I threw them both back. One of them almost died. He was on his back for a minute and then he came to and swam away."

Tommy is wearing a bright red sweatshirt and jean shorts. His blue eyes and blond hair stand out against it and against the bright green trees behind him. He is an advertisement for boyhood.

"Daddy, I'm hungry," he says.

We put away the fishing gear and head up to Jalapeno's Mexican Restaurant and Beach Mart. "Daddy, can I get some sunglasses?" he asks.

"If you really need them."

"Well, I just saw a pair I really like," he says.

He disappears, and then reappears over his quesadilla wearing a pair of oddly familiar dark glasses. They completely cover about a third of his face. He gives me a big smile and eats his quesadilla through his dark glasses.

"Daddy," he asks, "do these remind you of anyone?"

"Sort of."

"Don't I look just like you?" he asks. "Like you with your dark glasses?"

"You sure do." Amazingly, although he is blond and blue-eyed and has the world's tiniest nose, he does look like me. He has just willed *himself to look like me, as one might say.*

"See?" he says. "See?"

After the Mexican food, we race home. The wind is whipping through my fifty-one-year-old scalp, and Tommy is racing along behind me, pedaling furiously. Then he passes me on Second Street and laughs. I hunker down and pedal as hard as I dare. I catch up with him and pass him just as I get to our house. "Hey, no fair," he says. "No fair. You were really trying."

Amber, the stunningly beautiful local baby-sitter, comes over while I read documents for a trial and then take a nap. Afterwards, I can see Tommy and Amber throwing the Frisbee on the neighbor's glowing green lawn, lit up by the rain. "Look how well I can throw this, Daddy," he says as I watch through the window. "You have to keep it level. That's basic."

"Very impressive," I say.

Afterwards, Amber, Tommy, and I go for another bike ride, past Memorial Field, where the Sandpoint Summer Festival is setting up. There we see a few men with little bellies practicing their color guard drill to open the Festival. As Tommy watches, he says, "Very impressive."

Tommy wants to swim after his bike ride. It's raining again, but—what the heck—it's summer and he's eight. I watch him and Amber swim and play Frisbee in the water. Tommy has gotten so much taller since last summer that he is almost as tall as Amber, who is twenty. He's jumping in and out of the wavelets, leaping for the Frisbee. Behind them, enormous ducks with green markings are paddling back and forth, honking at one another. A mile away, I can see a green and white Burlington Northern freight train barreling across the rusted steel-grey railroad bridge over the Pend Oreille River where it enters Lake Pend Oreille. The sky is turning pink, and on the stereo Mary Chapin Carpenter is singing, "I feel lucky."

Tommy comes in and asks if he can get ice cream. "Why not?" It's summer and he's eight years old, wearing glasses that make him look just like Daddy.

TWO

In Hollywood there were once legendary hangouts of the stars. One thinks of black-and-white photos of Rita Hayworth at Ciro's, Clark Gable at the Mocambo, or Louis B. Mayer at Romanoff's. Those places are all gone now. There is only one power restaurant nightspot in Los Angeles. It's called Morton's, and it was founded in about 1978 by Peter Morton, scion of a wealthy Chicago family and founder of the Hard Rock Cafes.

Peter Morton has a twin sister named Pam who is the manager of Morton's. She became close friends with my wife about nine or ten years ago. Pam is as knowledgeable about how Los Angeles works as anyone I have ever met. She is, as they say, "wired." When she heard that our efforts to become parents had met with the frustration and fraud we should have seen coming, she suggested an adoption lawyer. The lawyer, she said, had a stellar record in finding sweet, lovely babies. His name was David Radis.

Alex and I went to see him in his unprepossessing offices in Century City. He was an intelligent, slightly disorganized-looking man who said he could probably help us. He had an interesting method: Alex and I would take out ads in various small town newspapers offering to adopt a woman's baby. The lawyer's many other hopeful parents would do the same. A little pool of babies would come into Radis's office. These would be distributed to the anxious parents according to how long they had been waiting.

It sounded farfetched to me, but we decided to give it a try. Within weeks, just as the ads began to run, Radis called us in. He had a break. A certain woman in a Midwestern state was pregnant. She had been pregnant before. She had given over a baby for adoption before. The baby had been healthy and cute. Another childless couple had been slated to have the new baby, but they had changed their minds. They were about eight years older than my wife and I were at that time, and they thought childrearing would be too much for them.

As I write this and think about the possibility that anyone else would have had our sweet boy, that he would not have been in my life and my wife's, I start to shake and sweat. (When I think of the millions like him ground up in abortions, I truly lose my mind.) At the time, of course, we had no idea how much we would love Tommy or what he would mean to me as a father. It was all *terra incognita* and extremely frightening.

"You can meet the mother," Radis said. "You can fly her out. All she needs is a plane ticket." When I think of what she has meant to us, I feel that I would have carried her out here on my back, but I did not know the future. We agreed to meet her, and we sent her a ticket. At the teeming TWA terminal at LAX airport, just weeks after first meeting David Radis, we watched breathlessly as the passengers deplaned. Hundreds of people came off that plane, but she did not show up. Nothing. Not there. My wife and I waited in the cavernous TWA terminal, feeling cheated and bitter. We felt so bereft that we went to a pound in Culver City and brought home a lost dog, a poor mutt we named Susan, to join the three we already had and to assuage our sorrow.

David Radis reported that the mother had gotten cold feet, nerves, fear of flying. He also told us that she was not the world's most reliable human being and that it was hard to predict what she might do next. Did we want to continue?

"No," I said. "Forget it. This woman is a wacko. The whole idea has bad karma around it."

"Absolutely yes," said my wife. "Don't even think about dropping it."

My wife is usually the diplomat's diplomat. For her to be so sure of anything and so determined was unheard of. Naturally, I "respected the parameters of the institution," as the saying goes at universities, and Alex got her way, thank God.

About a week later, we waited at the TWA terminal at LAX again. The very last person off the plane was a wan but attractive, surprisingly athletic-looking woman who was obviously pregnant. We knew who she was right away. The first thing she said was, "Am I allowed to smoke here in the terminal?"

She spent the weekend with us, staying at a hotel in Universal City. She went on the Universal Tour with the excitement of a small child. She came for a ride with us to Malibu but got carsick. She loved to smoke cigarettes.

We learned that she was already the mother of a lovely girl (she had pictures). She got pregnant by a man who was, as she said, "a minor league baseball player, home contractor, and con man." She also had a photo of him. He was a handsome fellow. The combination of athletic ability with the mental cunning and self-assurance needed to be a baseball player and con man struck us as perfect character and physical traits for modern life generally. The con man part fit into Hollywood particularly well.

The mother was unsophisticated but definitely not stupid. I sat with her at a Taco Bell in Malibu Canyon and asked her my favorite question from the 1961 booklet on preparing for the Scholastic Aptitude Test. "If two trains are three hundred miles apart on a straight line and they start at the same moment heading towards each other and the first train is going sixty miles per hour and the second train is going ninety miles per hour, how long until they pass each other?" She struggled with it on a napkin, and then I explained to her how to do it. Then I asked her about two boys reshelving library books after school at different rates of speed. In a flash she said, "That's the same question."

By the time she left, I was fond of her, and apprehensively ready to adopt her baby. We made the legal arrangements and started to send the checks. Those, by the way, were startlingly small. David Radis had arranged it so that we paid only the mother's usual living expenses, not any kind of large bounty. We made plans to buy furniture and to convert Alex's home office to a nursery.

That summer, we sublet an apartment in New York. In it I worked as ghostwriter on an autobiography of Jesse Jackson, one of the most impressive and strangest men I have ever met. (One example was his suggestion that I get to know him while he flew to Damascus to meet Hafez al-Assad and then on to Somalia to meet whoever the current gangster running the place was. He actually called our editor, Michael Korda, to suggest this over the phone while I was there. Korda came on the line to me and asked in a memorable seething hiss, "Are you insane?")

While I was in the New York sublet apartment, at 81st and York, asleep, I kept dreaming of how to rearrange the furniture in our tiny little house to allow room for our child. I never could figure out how to do it in my dreams. At the end of every dream, the baby was inside the house crying and I was outside on the street fuming.

In August of 1987, on the weekend just before the 16th, we went to the wedding of a beautiful young woman who had worked for us as a messenger. Although the woman had a lively past, she had arranged a true extravaganza of a white-gown wedding. Just as she said, "I do," a trained-dove handler released fifty doves into the Nichols Canyon sky. It was a humbling experience.

When we got home, there was a call from the mother of the mother of our baby. "You'd better get here," she said. "She's gone into labor."

With a chill running down my spine, I made arrangements for us to fly to Kansas City. By an odd coincidence, on the same flight we were on in lowly coach my wealthy cousin Jeffrey was on in first class. This seemed to me to reinforce the idea that parenthood was somehow a ticket to a second-class lifestyle. (I told you I was a fool.)

Alex and I drove through the unfamiliar Kansas City sprawl to Overland Park Hospital. By the time we got to the maternity ward, it was closed. Without any prompting by me, however, a nurse "recognized" me as a doctor and let us in. (I do look a lot like a doctor and often play one on TV.) We found our son in a clear plastic crib, looking small and cute but, as far as I could tell, much like any other child.

I was still apprehensive. I told Alex that we could still back out, and she just looked at me strictly.

Three days later, we were on a plane (in a state of shock) heading back to Los Angeles. I held Tommy on my lap and told him about the history of the world. He hardly cried at all.

When we got home, we found that our wonderful, stunningly capable assistant, Ann-Marie, had completely fixed up Tommy's nursery to look bright and cheerful and baby-ready. The baby nurse, a hearty older woman with amazingly strong hands, took the baby. Alex and the nurse began to talk animatedly about the baby. While I was on the phone, someone shut the door to the nursery. Bang, I was on the outside. As fast as you can say "knife."

I think it is commonplace for fathers of newborns to feel outside the loop. I recently worked on a TV commercial for eye drops where I had an Icelandic makeup woman. She told me that her husband had gone into shock when their baby came because he was no longer the center of attention. For me, the feeling was that I was ten thousand miles outside the loop, somewhere near Lower Slobbovia, a cipher, an errand boy whose main job was to go to the bank to get money to support my wife, the baby nurse, Tommy, and the dogs. It drove me wild. For example, without consulting me my wife had minor construction done on the house to build a closet for Tommy. In the process, a door to the backyard was sealed. This event, so incredibly trivial in retrospect, sent me into a total frenzy when it happened. I had bought that house before I had even planned to remarry Alex. It was my house. How could Alex order surgery on it without getting my permission?

At dinner the baby nurse sat with us (which struck me as strange), joined in the conversation, and lectured about proper nutrition, rest, and discipline—for Tommy. It was all too much attention to Tommy and all too little to me.

Then, about six weeks after Tommy's appearance, Joan Rivers sued me for libel over that humor piece about her in *GQ*. Since the article was not even remotely grounds for a libel suit, I was stunned. I expected *GQ*, a part of the mighty Condé

Nast empire, to step up to the plate with a vigorous defense of an article they had commissioned. After all, defending a major libel case is a giant expense for anyone except the likes of Condé Nast and is potentially devastating to an individual. But *GQ* was slow off the mark to step up to the defense, and their lawyers kept telling me they would not defend me at all. Plus, Joan Rivers had a lifetime accumulation of pals in the media. They never questioned whether there was a case. They only knew that their pal Joan had been hurt by, as she claimed, a former Nixon speech writer. Deciding which side they were on was child's play, especially for a witch at CBS named Kathleen Sullivan, who attacked me in almost unbelievably unfair terms, in my opinion.

I was completely flummoxed by the litigation, the expense, and the negative attention. Coming on top of the arrival of the baby, an event that seemed to push me right out of my own home, the Rivers lawsuit was a major upset.

Luckily, I had an ace researcher, the lovely and talented Susan Reifer, who found out some useful facts about the plaintiff and about certain death threats we had received. Susan's fabulous work, along with the resolution of my lawyer, Marty Singer—and with precious little help from mighty *GQ*—eventually got the lawsuit running on more equal terms. Eventually it was settled, with Joan Rivers apologizing to me and *GQ* for making negative implications about our honesty and integrity, with our saying we never doubted Joan was sad about her husband's death, and with a payment to a charity. That the case was ever filed still strikes me as incredible.

But while the case was new and in the news, I was still hard at work on Jesse Jackson's "autobiography." Even then it struck me as strange that I should be down in my basement office typing away on Jesse's rules for social justice while TV camera trucks and goofily dressed photographers waited for me on the street. I would write a passage to showcase some pithy phrase of the Reverend's about racism and self-reliance, and then the Friends of Joan Rivers would start beating on the door. (My favorite quote of Jesse Jackson's, which I frequently repeat to my son, is about work. "You can demonstrate and complain about white racism all you want," he would tell audiences, "and I will be there with you. But if you learn all the mathematics they teach in your school, you will always be able to feed your family. You can complain all you want about exclusion, and I'll help you complain. But if you learn how to plumb a house, you will always be able to feed your family and your children can go to college.")

Meanwhile, even though I, the Daddy, was the well-known one (in magazines and on talk shows), Tommy was always the one we were talking about at home. Tommy was the one we sang to. He was the one we carried around on our shoulders and bounced. He was the one we twirled around the swimming pool while we sang, *"Trot little horsie."* It did not seem right at all. I was bitter. I spent time at the beach. I spent time at restaurants with my Hollywood pals. I sulked.

It's amazing how much of my life can be summed up by saying, "I was a fool."

It was a blasting hot summer day in Malibu. Tommy and I were briefly home from North Idaho, during the same summer as the horrible incident on Alaska Airlines. Normally, the 'Bu has the most temperate and lovely of climates, but on this day the weather was cruelly hot. I was looking for lost checks in my basement in anticipation of my yearly torture-thon, known as income tax preparation, my files competing for space with spiders and dead mice. Tommy was building a paper airplane.

"Daddy, are we going to barbecue dinner tonight?" he asked.

"Yes, I think so."

"On the gas grill or the charcoal grill?"

"If it's working, on the gas grill."

"Why?"

"Because it's a lot easier to work with, plus gas is a lot cheaper to cook with than charcoal."

"Gas is cheaper than charcoal?" Tommy asked with a slightly condescending tone of disbelief.

"Yes, it is. By far."

"How can that be?" he asked.

"Because gas takes advantage of enormous advantages of scale in extraction and distribution—it's all very automated—while making charcoal and distributing it are still done by hand. That's why. Economies of scale. Doing a lot of something with machines rather than individual labor," said Daddy, the economist and son of an economist.

"Yes," Tommy, the grandson of an economist, shot back, "but you're ignoring the original cost of the gas grill. How much was it?"

"About two hundred and seventy dollars."

"And how much is charcoal?" asked little Alfred Marshall.

"Roughly ten dollars for a big bag that lasts a week."

"Then you'd have to use up twenty-seven bags of charcoal before you could even talk about the cost of making dinner tonight," said little Adam Smith, while his father's heart swelled with pride.

A few minutes later, we went to the Trancas Market to buy steaks for supper. I bought three while Tommy studied the video game counter. As we walked to the car, he asked, "Daddy, did you get three steaks?"

"Yes, I got three steaks, my boy," I said.

"Is one of them bigger than the others?"

"Yes."

"I want that one for my dinner," he said.

"No. You're the youngest and the smallest. Why should you have the biggest steak?"

"Because, Daddy, you're always saying I want to leave the table too fast. If I have a bigger steak to eat, if I eat at the same speed I usually do, I'll be at the table longer."

"Tommy, I am genuinely amazed. Your grasp of math concepts is superb. Truly superb. I am really delighted. If you wanted to, you could be a mathematician."

"Does that pay well?" he asked, somewhat deflating me.

"If you invent something that a lot of people use, it does. But it's a great, fascinating job anyway."

"If I invented something like Newton's Law of Gravity, would that pay well?"

"Newton didn't invent anything, sweetheart," I said. "He discovered *the law of gravity, but he didn't invent it. But if you discover a law like gravity, you'll be a god. You won't have to worry about anything. Money will be meaningless."*

"Good. In that case, I'd like to start tomorrow."

"Fine, Tommy. Just fine."

"But first I'll need a research grant. To buy supplies at Toys "R" Us."

THREE

By the spring of 1988, my jealousy of the baby and my feelings of being outside had reached desperation levels. Here I was, still in litigation, working madly by doing all different kinds of writing—fiction, exposés of fraud, notes on Hollywood life—and struggling to pay the bills, and when I got home, all I heard about was Tommy and all I saw was Tommy, who seemed to me still just a little bundle of screaming and crying and pooping. Once again, I had to "have my own space." If I could not get the attention that I, the king, was due, I would go and sulk like Achilles in his tent. I rented a little apartment on Malibu Beach Road, and soon I was spending all day there—and all night, too. It was my way of protesting all the attention paid to the infant Tommy instead of to me. It was my way of protesting the responsibilities of married life as a father. In retrospect, my behavior seems idiotic, although it was motivated by concerns and feelings that were far from idiotic. Human jealousy is not a null quantity and is fairly evenly distributed over the human spectrum, as far as I can tell. Wanting to have attention paid is also neither insane nor stupid. However, spending so much time away from home was, in hindsight, a big error. The problem might have been fixed by some sense of humor on my part and by some understanding of what I was going through on Alex's part, but it wasn't. So, instead of spending time with my boy at one of his cutest stages, I typed madly by myself out at the beach. That may sound romantic and writerly. In fact, it was just lonely. There are few places in a big city as desolate as Malibu in winter (or spring or fall).

Three facets of my life kept me from complete self-imposed stir-craziness. First, my wife, God bless her, would often bring Tommy out to visit me, even though we were in fact largely separated, and I often went into town to see him. It was very much a *pro forma* thing, and I certainly felt little connection with the baby. If I did feel anything, it was apprehension about what his presence might deprive *me* of next, guilt about how badly my absence was probably hurting *him,* and bewilderment over how I ever got into the position of being such a bad father. In other words, my attitude toward Tommy was based on anger and self-loathing and anxiety.

Second, I was teaching at Pepperdine. I had taught about the law of libel for years at Pepperdine, and I added a class on the politics of mass culture. It was great to be around the young students. They reinforced my delusional notion that there was still some star quality about me, that I, not a small infant, was properly the study of mankind.

Third, I joined several 12-step groups. I did it largely because I was so lonely and depressed about my life. Friends, in particular, a woman in Alexandria, Virginia, told me I would fit in a 12-step group and be happy there. About fifteen minutes from me in an unused school building in a neighborhood called Point Dume (pronounced "doom," as in one's doom or one's fate), there was a noon meeting of a 12-step group. Off I went. I did not want to drink, use drugs, overeat, or overspend, so I could honestly fit into the groups.

Next to my relationship with my son, probably the 12-step meetings opened my eyes to the possibilities of life more than anything else that has ever been in my life. The Program, as it was called, was not really about quitting drinking or anything else. It was about developing a whole new way of life. This way of life called for admission of one's faults, surrender to the power of God, and a drastic effort to make one's life simpler, a requirement that when in disputes, I consider that I was wrong. The Program taught that straightforward adherence to the basic rules of life is right. The Program taught me that my responsibilities to my fellow human beings did not enslave me but freed me. It taught me that when I am upset and sulking about something, it is usually because I am trying to control life—an impossible task—instead of just settling down and living life on life's terms.

In the meetings—held in a little, poorly repaired room looking out on a magnificent green park—we talked about how in life there are no big deals except one. The only big deal is maintaining one's sense of serenity and surrender to God.

All of this might have sounded touchy-feely or feel-good or otherwise unsophisticated to me at other times in my life. But in the fall of 1988, it sounded exactly right. It was what I needed to hear. My life and my behavior towards my family were so wildly off-plumb that I needed basic lessons in how to live, especially in relation to God. The realization I came to at the 12-step meetings—that I was not the boss, that I was only a staff member of a huge enterprise whose Chief Executive demanded obedience and respect for His laws—was key in rebuilding all of my relationships.

I can vividly recall sitting in a meeting and listening to ex-cons, probationers, and car thieves talk about how they had found some peace in their lives. They made much more sense than most of the super-high-end shrinks I had seen off and on for twenty years. The 12-step folks certainly made more sense to me than I had been making to myself.

"Feelings come and feelings go," said a plump woman, "and feelings are not facts." This statement in itself revolutionized my thinking.

"Sometimes just doing the simple, conventional thing instead of your own fancy version is the right way to go," said a very thin woman.

"When in doubt or anxiety, pause, rest, and do the right thing," said a local plumber.

"Turn it over to God, and stop trying to be in control," said an unemployed salesman.

"If you want to improve the movie of your life, fire yourself as the director," said a visiting music producer.

"If you have trouble sleeping, make a list of all the things in your life that are truly fabulous that you do not deserve," said a surfer. "Then make a list of your friends."

One of the major turning points in the story of Tommy and me came from a woman in the 12-step program named J. At one meeting I was talking, as I often did, about how I went for walks in the Point Dume area (I had moved there by then, as a lowly renter). In my usual sick, jealous way, I was talking about how I took my son on weekend days and looked at the houses of the rich and felt as if they were better than mine. I talked about how envious and bitter that made me feel. J., who had seen me walking with Tommy in his stroller and had seen me pushing him endlessly on the swings at Point Dume Park (I was always good for pushing him for long periods, and that turned out to be good training for being a father), asked, "Did you ever think that other people might have better houses than you do but no one has a better son than you do?" Her question stunned me. "You have a gorgeous, beautiful son. Why don't you concentrate on being happy about that? You also have an incredibly beautiful dog. Concentrate on those two."

This started me thinking that maybe I had everything upside down. Was it possible, at least a little bit possible, that Tommy was not a burden but a privilege? Could it be that I had made a mistake as basic as that? Could I, lowly scum-of-the-earth-at-the-center-of-the-universe me, possibly have a future made richer and better by my son? It was worth thinking about.

When I saw Tommy on the weekends, he was scared of me. He did not like my taking him anywhere but the swings. He cried when I took him to the supermarket at Point Dume. I vividly recall carrying Tommy to the back of my huge rented garden to look at hummingbirds. He shrieked with fear at being in the overgrown brush far from his mother. "Why are you crying?" I asked him. "I'm not doing anything bad to you." He just kept crying, and I felt as if I were a serial killer. And when I corrected Tommy for misbehavior, he would just lie on his stomach motionlessly and stare at the puke-green carpet.

Maybe close father–son stuff was just not meant for me. But it hurt me that Tommy and I were estranged. It hurt Tommy, too. In fact, Tommy's upset at being around me was just one small part of his general behavior problems. In school (he was by then in preschool at Temple Israel of Hollywood) he cried much more than the other kids. He was short-tempered and picked fights. The mother of one of his classmates, a woman who claimed to be a psychologist, said he had attention deficit disorder. She said he was hyperactive and "not wired like other kids."

One day when I picked Tommy up at preschool, he shrank to a corner of the room and cried. He continued crying as I carried him to the car. He only stopped crying when I took him to a video store and let him pick out a video. Clearly, something was extremely wrong: I was out at the beach feeling miserable, Tommy was in town feeling miserable, and Alex, my long-suffering bride, was patient but not happy about Tommy's course of development. I assumed she was miserable about Tommy's situation, too. Once, when I visited briefly and then got into my mighty black BMW to drive back to Malibu, she walked me to the car and said, "I just cry at night sometimes thinking about Tommy growing up without a father there for him all the time."

Walking through Beverly Hills with Tommy one Saturday afternoon, I saw a film producer whom I knew fairly well walking up Rodeo Drive with his son, who was about Tommy's age, sitting on his shoulders and looking proud and happy and confident. I was holding the trembling hand of a still-fearful Tommy. *Why,* I thought to myself, *why? Why am I such a poor, inadequate excuse for a father?* Even one of the girls I occasionally hired to file told me that while I was kind and generous to her, she marveled that I did not have a better relationship with my son. "How can someone as smart as you and as thoughtful to the people who work for you be such a bad father?"

On another weekend a movie producer and ace casting guy named Michael Chinich, the man who first put me in a movie, came over to see us. He brought Tommy a huge kiddie car. When Tommy climbed into it, Michael got down on the floor and played with him, pushing the car around the room. He and Tommy whooped with joy together as the car crashed into sofas and love seats and dogs. *Why?* I thought. *Why can't I break through whatever is between me and Tommy and play on the floor with him the way Chinich does? Why can't I scream with laughter and delight with my boy the way Chinich does with him? Is it because I feel jealous of the attention paid to him? Is it because I feel guilty about how much I have neglected him? Is it because I am so bowed down by low self-esteem that I cannot imagine taking on the manly role of father? Why?*

I had learned in my 12-step program that right acting often preceded right thinking. Some kind of right acting was needed and needed soon. Father–child problems cannot be allowed to go on forever, or, as one might say, they go on forever. I had to start acting like a father or "it" would never happen.

The breakthrough in right acting began one night when I had to buy a new TV set for my wife. I was at her house measuring the space where the TV would go when Tommy walked in with a little child's measuring tape and started to measure the same spot himself. It was adorable. He has always loved tools and loves to be the workman. When I got down on the floor to look for the cable outlet, he got a flashlight and shined it on the spot. "Why don't you take him with you to Circuit City," Alex said. "He has a different personality with everyone he's with. He'll start developing more of a special personality with you."

"I'm scared," I said. "I've never taken him anywhere with me at night."

"You'll be fine," Alex said.

Tommy cried like a madman when I put him in the car. He cried like a madman when I drove down Outpost Drive with him. I can still recall his shrieks of terror or resistance or whatever it was. But when we got to the store, his fear vanished. Curiosity and a sense of the new and exciting replaced it. Tommy ran around the banks of TVs in pure ecstasy. He played with the buttons. He changed the channels. He screamed with joy. He was making so much noise and disturbing the TVs so much the manager complained, a sure sign that a twenty-two-month-old child is having a great time. We bought a little Sony. Tommy "helped" put it in the trunk by touching it after it was in the cavernous space. He sang some incomprehensible nursery rhyme he had learned from the TV on the way home. He was happy.

That night Tommy "helped" me install the TV. Finally, we got it to work. Then we watched a show on it—one of his "learning tapes"—about a group of kids playing with a clown on a train. Then I put him in his crib, and I told him a story. Note that even before, when I was around, I always told him stories. I also sang to him. I also pushed him back and forth in his car and twirled him around in the swimming pool until I thought I would puke. The problem was not that I acted like Jack The Ripper when I was with him; it was that I was not with him enough. The story I told him that night was probably about dogs. He was wild about dogs, perhaps out of necessity since there were always at least three, and sometimes four, large dogs around; we had two German shorthaired pointers, a weimaraner, and a pitiful mutt. The whole house was like a large doghouse wrapped around two and a half humans (I was the half) and the dogs. In fact, as far as I know, at that time the only words Tommy could say were "dog" and "cat."

I stood over the crib as I finished the story (which probably ended with the dog selling a screenplay and achieving fame and position in the Hollywood community) and looked at Tommy's little face with his blond curls. "All right," I said, since I thought he was asleep. "Good night, my boy." I said it with real feeling, since I felt that we had just spent a good evening together and that maybe there was hope for us after all. Tommy opened his glowing light blue eyes and looked at me. "Good-night, Daddy," he said with perfect pitch and enunciation. He said it so calmly and with so much conviction and poise that it sounded to me that he had just said, "I love you, Daddy, and I always have and I always will, no matter what. And your life means something."

Tommy spent his last birthday in single digits with me in Sandpoint, Idaho, that same summer. The night before, I told him that he could buy anything he wanted at the local Wal-Mart. He ran up and down the aisles of the toy section. He ran into the Nerf gun section and started hauling down various guns like a starving man finding loaves of bread. The Perceptor, the T-3, the Stinging Scarab, the Snapping Crocodile, the Autogrip—all of them fell into his cart. Then he returned the Perceptor and got credit for a future Nerf gun. Tommy's pals Alex and Jake spent the night with us at our rented house. They ran around the house shooting each other with Nerf darts. Every few minutes Tommy would grab me as I sat reading e-mail. "You can't shoot me when I'm with Daddy," he told his pals. "When I'm holding Daddy, I'm safe."

Because it was a warm night, my son's baby-sitter, Amber, came over later. We all—kids, baby-sitter, and I—went out in the dim moonlight on my boat. We cruised slowly out of the marina, then floored it to get up on plane, and roared across the neck of the Pend Oreille River, then across to Contest Point, past Sourdough Point, and into Bottle Bay. We got hamburgers at the marina there, then headed back in brighter moonlight to Sandpoint again. I let Tommy turn on the halogen light on the front of the boat so he and his friends could see the billions of bugs hovering over the water and watch as the kokanee salmon broke the surface to eat them. Then I let Tommy drive, with me millimeters away. He grinned and then concentrated intently, his little brow furrowed, as he maneuvered us into port. He was happy. I let his pals drive the boat. They were happy. They jumped up and down and squealed with delight as we hit the wakes of other boats out for a nighttime cruise. When I took the wheel again, Tommy held his arms around my neck tightly, pulling it towards him. "Watch it, my boy," I said. "I'm driving."

"I'm holding on to you forever," he said. "I'm never letting you go."

"I have to hold my head up to steer the boat," I said. "I have to be able to see if there are logs out there. I have to be able to keep us afloat."

"I'll keep us afloat, too," Tommy said. "We'll both keep the boat afloat."

I felt as if a hot fire were burning inside me, lighting up my insides. In 1962, as I was walking past the Waldorf Astoria, I saw a limousine dropping off President John F. Kennedy at that grand hotel. He looked, as my companion said at the time, as if he had lights inside him. That's how I felt as we rounded Contest Point.

Years ago, when I was a child of nine, we had a neighbor named Dave Scull. He was a real estate agent, a Princeton man, a war hero, a sometime Republican candidate for local office—and a great guy. He had much of the child in him even in his early forties. One summer night he came home with a slightly used Lincoln convertible. He loaded his son and daughter and me into it and drove us around the streets amidst masses of fireflies. It was a gilded, glowing night, like a night from a Fellini movie. Sitting in the backseat of Mr. Scull's 1953 Lincoln as we rode down a suburban street, I felt like a returning war hero. This was, after all, almost the same car that Ike and Dick had ridden to their inauguration not long before.

Now, *I thought to myself as we slowed to "no wake" on Lake Pend Oreille and entered our slip,* I am the Mr. Scull of this group, at least tonight. *The bright lights of the Sandpoint Marina were like the lights that Fellini always had on his beaches, replacing the fireflies of 1954.*

We went to get pizza at the local Pizza Hut, had birthday cake, and then came home. Tommy's pals went to sleep in the bunk beds in his room. Tommy wanted to sleep in bed with me, as usual, but before he went to bed, he said, "I'm hungry. I want some tomato soup."

"No," I said. "You had pizza. You had cake. You had hamburgers. I'm tired. Happy birthday. Good night."

"But I'm hungry," he said.

"All right." I went downstairs and made him tomato soup. He ate it and then wanted apple pie. "Garfield is full now," he said as he got into bed. When Tommy is in a good mood, he pretends he is Garfield, the cartoon cat.

"Good, Garfield," I said. "Go to sleep so we can take you and your pals to laser tag tomorrow."

"No, Garfield has to sharpen his claws on you." He scratched his fingers on me for a few seconds and then lay across me. "Garfield wants to sleep like this," he said. "Garfield wants to sleep on your chest until it's time to go play laser tag."

"All right, Garfield."

Tommy lay with his head on my shoulder. "Garfield says if you move him, he'll call nine-one-one and tell them it's child abuse. If you move me off you, it's child abuse. So, pooh, and you have to let me sleep with my head on you all night 'cause it's my birthday."

After Tommy fell asleep, I moved him to his side of the bed and put a huge pillow between us to keep him from kicking me in his sleep, one of his great unconscious pleasures. But when I awakened in the middle of the night, he was sleeping with his head on my other shoulder and his hand across my chest. This time I didn't move him, because if I had, it would have been child abuse.

FOUR

As I pondered my situation with Mr. Perfect, Tommy Stein, I realized that he had indeed thrown the door to his affection open that night when he said "Good night, Daddy" so sweetly. But could I walk through it? The problem, in part, was that I had such low self-esteem, such a miserable feeling about myself, that I wondered how Tommy could possibly love me. I had not really succeeded in Hollywood. I was not rich, certainly not even close by Hollywood standards. I had been a miserable father for Tommy's first few years. How could I ever feel that my son could love me for very long? I was poor at athletics as a youth, and no better as an adult. What could ever make Tommy love me? And if he did not love me, how could I spend time with him? How humiliating it would be to have a son who held me in contempt, open or secret.

I thought about this for a few days and then I heard something on the radio that really stunned me. A man named Dr. James Dobson, a Christian minister out of Colorado, had little snippets that came on the local all-news station, KNX. In one that I heard as I drove across the mountains between Malibu and the Simi Valley, he was talking about a father who felt that he did not have the ability to love his kids. He felt as if he had been a failure in his life, and he lacked the capacity to be a loving father because he had so little love for himself.

Dr. Dobson, a man with an engaging country accent, said something to this effect: Your children look up to you and idolize you no matter what the rest of the world thinks of you. Your children are a bottomless reservoir of affection and esteem for you if you will just spend time with them and tap that reservoir. If you did not have self-esteem before, spending time with your kids, allowing them to lavish their adoration on you, and feeling how strongly they need you will give you exactly that sense of affection for yourself that you need. You can then give it back to them in spades and get still more affection and admiration from them. If the problem keeping you from spending a lot of time with your kids is self-esteem, spending time with your kids will give you exactly what you need. The solution, he said, is contained within the problem, and once you start solving it, it continues to solve itself.

That very weekend I did something brave. I took Tommy out to my home in Malibu all by myself. I had made a vow that I would never do it, because I was so frightened that I would do it wrong and wind up with him crying himself into a coma. But how would I ever get close to him if we could not be in my home by ourselves?

Tommy screamed like a banshee when I put him in the car. He screamed and cried until we got onto the Hollywood Freeway. Then he kept screaming. I was at the point of bringing him back when I had a great idea. Employing the full power of the broadcast medium, playing off the whole culture of youth, I said to him, "Tommy, would you like to go to Toys "R" Us?" He stopped crying immediately and off we went down Topanga Canyon Boulevard to Toys "R" Us. I had diverted him with an application of the drug of toys that the TV had been selling him all his life.

For the rest of the afternoon, I was on the floor with him pushing back and forth various toys. In fact, he was so happy playing with his fire truck, or whatever it was, that he completely forgot how frightened he had been to be with his somewhat distant father. On the way back, the little demon even recognized the area and demanded to go to Toys "R" Us again. (We did, thus beginning a pattern of compulsive shopping by Mr. Perfect that continues to this day and will probably continue after I die. In every sense, shopping is his drug. He gets it from his parents. And from my late mother. Compared with many other drugs, it's harmless.)

Tommy's screams of protest on our drives to Malibu continued for about a month after our first trip there. There would be tears and wailing until we reached Toys "R" Us. Then we would have toy buying. Then we would have nudging about McDonald's because, as luck would have it, a brand-new McDonald's went up right on the route to Malibu just as I began to bring him out there. Then we would have Happy Meal buying, with Tommy throwing away the food and playing with the toy in the package. I marveled at how McDonald's was able to sell food at a staggering price per ounce of meat by including a few square centimeters of dyed plastic. I marveled at how many of us parents were there in Toys "R" Us and McDonald's bribing our kiddies with vile "action figures" and fast food. Much of parenting of very small children is bribing them, drugging them with toys and food, I swiftly realized.

I am sure there are parents who refuse to be swayed by a child's pleas for a G.I. Joe action figure or a remote control car. There are probably parents who are strong enough to make their kids suffer for their political and social predilections, to deprive them now to make them strong later. Frankly, I do not have that much strength. My mind is too weak to deal with a crying son for very long unless I know the tears are totally phony—as they often are—and then I can deal with them for a long, long time.

But if my son genuinely wants something, I like to give it to him. As I ransack my memory and as I consult with other parents, I cannot find many episodes or examples of children ruined by having too many toys. The children I see who are wrecked do not look as if they have had too much—but far too little. I would really love to see some documentation of whether or not buying a lot of toys in fact ruins kids. I suspect this theory has a very modest basis in fact.

Or, to put it as an economist would, for a few dollars I can get a few hours of peace of mind and a happy, smiling Tommy. At most, the buying has a neutral effect on Tommy's well-being. If he is going to grow up demolished, God forbid, it is not going to be because he had too many Nerf guns but because he did not feel he had a place in the universe. If it's at all possible, I am going to make him feel as if he does have such a place. If doing that keeps him quiet, so much the better.

At Toys "R" Us, I also saw how very easy it is to seem like a parent. I would cruise up the bike aisle and down the remote control aisle at Toys "R" Us looking weary and put upon, even if I really felt pretty good. (I find the array of toys at bargain prices beguiling as well as overwhelming.) With their children nearby, parents of all nationalities—Laotians in saffron robes, Chinese in loose-fitting smocks, Africans in colorful robes, ordinary, very large Americans in stretch pants—would walk past, all looking similarly weary and put upon. An international fraternity of parents and demanding kids formed at Toys "R" Us.

I was in the club on the first trip. The other parents didn't know of my conflicts and fears and failures. They didn't care who I was or was not in Hollywood. To them, I was just another patient parent. Just sighing as I subtly motioned to all of my son's uneaten food at Mickey D's made me one of the fathers in anguish over his kid's waste of his hard-earned money (*Middle-class child* in America is a synonym for *stunning waster of everything*). The others didn't know that I was living by myself and that my son cried when he got into the car—*and they didn't care.* We were all just parents together. (We would all worry a lot less about what other people think of us if we realized how rarely they do so, as the saying goes, and this is true of the parents of the world as well. No Maureen Dowd lurks waiting to expose us all in the *New York Times.* We are just schleppers, beneath much notice except our own.)

When we got out to Malibu after the first few times, Tommy took up a routine. It involved a staggering amount of time spent watching TV cartoons—*Rugrats* (a good one), *Ren and Stimpy* (a very good one), *Real Monsters* (or maybe they came later), *Donald Duck* (punching Hirohito in reruns from 1944), *Roadrunners* (ancient), and dearly beloved *Rocky and Bullwinkle* cartoons that Alex and I had watched in New Haven. Cartoons until you wanted to cry. Interlaced with ads for cereals, dolls, action figures, guns, remote control trucks—everything that kids want and need, beyond counting.

Then Tommy started to watch videotapes of Israelis teaching children to play (it must be taught in Israeli schools that Israelis can teach anyone to do anything). And videos of spiders and reptiles (these were a special favorite of my son's). Then more cartoons. Then silly live-action shows on Nickelodeon. Then a medical channel where they show operations, complete with blood and cartilage (Tommy loved those in particular). Outside it would be dazzling, bright blue, beautiful. Inside we would be watching my TV, while Trixie, the German shorthaired pointer, snored on the bed.

I would bring Tommy out to help me garden around my pitiful, perpetually struggling jacarandas. He would cry that he was missing a cartoon. I would take him for a walk to a broad Malibu vista over the mighty blue Pacific, looking far out to Catalina. He did not like it and wanted to go back home. He wanted to watch a video about snakes for the tenth time (amazingly, he liked the video and so did I, no matter how many times we watched it).

In about 1985, before we had Tommy, my wife and I had a visit from our pals from Yale, Dick and Eileen Balzer. They had their kids in tow and were heading off for a visit to Disneyland, a spot of limited appeal to the Balzers. I asked the Balzers why they were going to a place they disliked. Eileen Balzer looked at us with the pity reserved for the truly ignorant. "When you're a parent, you'll do things with your kids that you never would have dreamed you'd do. What's more, you'll do them and you'll love doing them."

As I made Tommy hot chocolate (and was happy to do it if he would only drink it), as I sat with him while he watched Goofy and Minnie, as I watched detailed descriptions of the different kinds of poisons carried by various snakes (and learned something new each time, and hated it each time, but also loved it because it brought peace and a smile to my son's face), I realized how true Eileen's words were.

Then, a breakthrough in the struggle for the soul of Tommy Stein: One night when it was time for me to bring him back to Hollywood to see Mom, he did something new; he asked me if he could stay longer at my house in Malibu. He wanted to watch still more cartoons, to get a still larger fix of animation. He wanted to watch *Nick at Nite* live shows, too. Someone named Clarissa and two boys named Pete had a special hold on his soul, as did some dancers on a show called *Roundhouse.*

I was not a huge fan of these shows. But whatever Tommy might have thought he was asking for, he was also asking to spend more time with me. Maybe he was also with Clarissa and Pete and Pete, but he was still with me. If he had been terrified of me, if he had hated being with me, he would have just wanted to go home to Mommy as soon as possible. He wanted to stay out at the beach with Daddy. Moreover, if he stayed to dusk or beyond, he wanted to sit right next to me, and often wanted to lean against me. He was scared of the dark (he is still scared of the dark). He saw Daddy as the Protector Against the Dark. This was a major coup for me. It had been a long time, if ever, since anyone had seen me as Protector Against Basic Fears. I guess I was a protector against economic insecurity (which is the root meaning of *husband*—"protector and caretaker of the house") for my wife until she became a major Hollywood lawyer. But she very well knew that neither I nor anyone else could protect her against the really dark aspects of human existence. Tommy thought I could. He thought that if he stayed with me and stayed close to me, he was protected against whatever might be scaring him, whatever unknowable danger was out there.

It is hard to exaggerate how good this made me feel. To the powers of Hollywood studioland, who specialize in lowering self-esteem, I was a nobody; I was a writer and character actor, the lowest forms of creation. To the billionaire subjects of my articles, I was a gnat, barely worth the effort to swat at. But to Tommy Stein, I was the guy he had to be close to in the dark. When we arrived at my house in Malibu at night,

Tommy had to literally hold on to my trousers as I walked from room to room turning on the lights. If it was after dusk, Tommy had to be with me, sitting right next to me as I worked on the computer, as I filed, as I paid bills. I was life-and-death indispensable to him after it got dark. It would be impossible to express how big this made me feel.

Then came the matter of athletics. I had been afraid that Tommy would think poorly of me because I was such a poor athlete (I envisioned a young Ty Cobb or Cal Ripken tearing around the bases while I plodded along pitifully behind him). Of course, when he was three, Tommy was a far worse athlete than I was. I would take him to Point Dume Park and pitch foam balls at him, and he would miss them. Then I would take the same balls, toss them in the air, and whack them. Tommy would look at me with amazement and delight and even awe. I have always lifted weights in my own fashion. Even though the weight I hoisted was a feather by Schwarzenegger standards, to Tommy it was like lifting a freight car. He would watch me lift a bar twenty times, a bar he could not budge at all. He was impressed. Not only that, but he said he was impressed. "You are so strong," he would say. "Will I be that strong when I grow up?"

"Yes, much, much stronger," I would say. "You'll be able to lift me up with one hand."

"Really, Daddy?"

Tommy's appreciation of Daddy's very limited strength and athletic ability and his belief that Daddy could protect him against what lurked in the dark were proof of what I had heard from Dr. Dobson on the radio: To a child of three or four, a father who spends time with him is a god. To Tommy Stein, I was Charles Atlas, Einstein, and Superman all put together. I realized that if I paid attention to him, if I were in fact his protector, his admiration for me would be limitless. If I was there for him, he was there for me in redoubled spades. However secure or accompanied I made him feel, that is one-tenth of how big he made me feel.

Another giant breakthrough came when there was some special kind of *Nick at Nite* marathon. It had been advertised relentlessly on Nick all day on Saturday. (When Nick advertises, they are the Curtis LeMay of advertising. They have an understanding of what selling means that George Washington Hill would have envied. They carpet bomb the viewer so that his morale crumbles and his thoughts turn to watching whatever Nick commands.) The show that was being advertised was unusual. Not only did it go on until late at night, by Tommy's standards, but it also had ads for a new series of cartoons that started the next morning. Plus, it had some ads for soup. Tommy formed a new idea: "Daddy, can I stay here until this is over and then watch the other shows in the morning? And can I have some tomato soup for dinner?"

I really could have cried. I called Alex. She was not jealous. She was delighted that Tommy was getting close to the daddy she had feared he would never know. "Of course, my boy," I said to him. "Of course you may stay. We'll go down to the Trancas Market and get you some soup right this minute."

From a standing start, when Tommy cried as I took him to Circuit City, within a few months—with the good help of Toys "R" Us, McDonald's, Dr. Dobson, and the mighty TV—my son's attitude had completely changed. He did not want to flee home to Mom. He wanted to spend the night with me in Malibu, a wish I had not expected to see for years, if ever.

Time is a thief, so I cannot recall exactly what happened that night. I do know that I just asked Tommy as I was writing this what we did that night. "We watched *Ren and Stimpy,*" he said. "Don't you remember? You were the one who taught me to watch it and love it. It used to be on late Saturday nights and also early Sunday mornings, around ten. Now it's only on Sunday mornings." I do recall that I made Tommy his soup and toast (and probably French toast as well). I might also have made him Shake 'n Bake chicken. I recall feeding him and watching him slurp it all up. He would ask for more, like an orphan from Charles Dickens, and I would always make him more.

There is some special feeling about doing something that pleases your child. Feeding Tommy has always been a special pleasure for me. I just love to make him more and more food until he says he has had enough. It is a total myth that only women like to nurture by feeding. I love to feed my boy (and now that I have friends with small children, I like to feed them as well). In daily life so much of what I do is of indirect or questionable benefit that when I can find something to do that is of unquestionable and clear value, I want to do it. If it's of unquestionable value to my one and only son, I really am deeply eager to do it. That is real status in my little world: to do right for your child.

Further, there are only so many things that I can unequivocally do correctly. I can feed my son such that he is full and adequately (if not perfectly) nourished. This makes me happy. But of course it's not just an issue of logic. There is something primally gratifying about feeding my son. It's almost like seeking sex or making money. It's innate.

As I look back on this turning point, I am amazed at how easy it was to earn Tommy's trust. He was not suspicious or watchful at all. I attribute that to his having been smothered with attention from birth, so that he was naturally disposed to feel that he would get attention and love from everyone, even from the father whose appearance once made him cry. Perhaps he was also predisposed to be comfortable around me because although I had not been around him as much as I should have been, I was around him regularly. Plus, his mother and I almost never fought in his presence.

Or maybe kids are just programmed to love their daddies, just as their daddies are programmed to feed them and love doing it. Maybe nurture is a part of nature, and so is loving your mom and dad, even if they are middle-aged and filled with self-doubt. *What*ever, as the friends of Tommy Stein say. I do recall that when I fed Tommy, lay in bed with him until he fell asleep, felt him snuggle against me in unconsciousness, and looked out the window with him at the airpianes coming into LAX, I had a wonderful feeling that humans rarely get: of being in the exactly right place. Being with my son as Protector Against the Dark was the best job I have ever had. No stock options but a lot of prestige and job satisfaction.

Children have moods. Children as fantastically catered to as Tommy Stein have extremely notable, obvious moods. On a Saturday in October of 1996, after a Saturday morning soccer game, Tommy went into a major sulk. He had wanted to buy yet another remote control car—after getting the most expensive one in the catalogue the day before. I said enough was enough, and he sulked. Now it would be easy for me to say that I said some magic words to get him to change his mood, but I didn't. Instead, when we got to our house in Malibu, I just told him the truth—that I was exhausted—and told him to amuse himself with his box of toys and games. I fell asleep and when I awoke, Tommy's bad mood had vanished. He was playing with his powerful remote control toy in the driveway. He was happy. He could not remember why he had been upset. Then the battery of the car ran out. He had forgotten the recharger, so he was left to rely on non–remote control toys. He got out some old remote control toys, fiddled with them, inserted new batteries, and soon had other cars to play with.

When Tommy saw that I was awake, he came in and took off my stereo headphones. "Daddy," he said, "come race cars with me."

"I can't," I said. "I have pleurisy in my lung. I don't feel at all well."

"But, Daddy," he pleaded. "I don't want to play lonely all by myself."

Hearing that your child is lonely and has to "play lonely" by himself is like getting electroconvulsive therapy. It is like adding electricity to Frankenstein's monster. No matter how sick you feel, you must drag yourself out of bed and play with that child of yours, lest he grow up feeling lonely all by himself.

Tommy wanted to go to a nearby beach and dig a hole and hide in it. "Why?" I asked. "What's the point?"

"Simulating trench warfare," he said blithely.

"But we won't be shooting at each other," I said.

"That makes it better than trench warfare."

We took a spade to the beach, and I started to dig his hole. Within minutes it was deep enough for him to hunker in so that only the top of his towhead was visible. "Daddy, I'm hiding," he said. "Do you see me?"

"I see you."

It was late in the afternoon. Except for the lifeguard, there was no one on the beach. In the water were about a dozen surfers; they rode the waves like ballet dancers, with a sense of balance that is a gift. Tommy ran up and down the beach, occasionally hiding behind a rock, occasionally tossing seaweed at me, occasionally darting into the cold waves and then running out. He smiled as if his mouth would crack open. The silent, sulking Tommy who had refused to have lunch two hours earlier had vanished.

"Do we have to go?" Tommy asked after about a half hour.

"We can stay as long as you want."

"Why?" he asked. "You're usually in a hurry to get back and file."

"Because this is where I'm supposed to be this afternoon." I sat on a concrete step and watched my son run around. I saw him struggle with an immense log that had washed ashore. He was happy. He was playing, but he was no longer by himself. He was an accompanied minor. But the giver was getting the gift. It was the best time I have ever had on a beach.

In the car on the way back, Tommy asked if he could have a brownie and orange soda. I took him to the Trancas Market to get them. He also bought yogurt, ice cream, candy bars, and sliced turkey. "I feel hungry, Daddy," he said. "When we get home, let's have dinner while we watch Ren and Stimpy, *and then you tell me about what the beach was like when you were young."*

"It was lonely."

"Why?"

"Because I didn't have you to play with. I had to play lonely by myself."

"Is that a joke?" Tommy asked.

"Not in the least."

When I got home, I had a mountain of data to study on who is considered rich in the land of 1996-stock-market-boom

America. Is it those with a household net worth of $5 million? Those families with a per person net worth of $1.3 million? Those with taxable income of $500,000 or more?

I think I have a better way to measure it.

FIVE

Conflict is a bad thing when it's happening inside my brain. It is extremely hard for me to bring all of my personality and self to bear on any issue if I have some civil war raging inside my brain.

Low self-esteem is a bad thing, at least when it's happening to me or anyone I love. Low self-esteem makes it hard for me to bring much high esteem to any situation in which I am a party or to any person around me.

Earning a living is a difficult concept to reconcile with the two above if earning a living means trying to sell scripts or be a producer in Hollywood.

The process of selling scripts (never easy for me except for a brief stretch of about six years) had become excruciatingly horrible by the late 1980s. Pitching story lines was a synonym for humiliation. When I first came to Hollywood, in 1976, I sold to men and women older than I was, with some modicum of experience. If they turned me down, as they often did, they did so for a reason or set of reasons that often made sense to me. I can remember leaving pitch meetings thinking that I had learned something beyond the value of humility.

But by, say, 1990, the pitch meeting was pure self-immolation, far worse than it had ever been before. The script development meeting was even deadlier. I can vividly recall a cruel meeting in 1990 with a woman who had just been promoted from receptionist at a small production company to "vice president for development" of that company. She complained that a draft I had written did not fully explain what happened between scenes.

"That's called ellipsis," I said. "It's a literary or poetic device."

"Well, I don't like it," she said. "I want to know everything that happens."

"Well, let me ask you something," I replied. "Do you think a script should be more like instructions for operating a copier or like a poem?"

"It's got to be like instructions for operating a copier," she said.

I searched her face in vain for any sign that she might be joking.

I can recall a dinner meeting with a famous producer who wanted me to write a script about the return of Thomas Jefferson to modern-day America and what he might think of what's going on. "Great," I said. I was really impressed. "So he can comment on things like big government and quotas and be amazed at the progress of black America?"

"Yes, and mostly so he can teach people that it's good to smoke hemp. He was a major-league pot smoker. That's the point I want to get across."

"You want a movie that teaches young people that Jefferson would think it's a good thing to smoke reefer?"

"Exactly," said the producer.

When I told him I would not do it under any circumstances, he backed off on the dope angle and hired me anyway. "He's just going to get someone else to rewrite it and put in the pot stuff later," a mutual friend explained. It was the only job I had that year, and I took it.

Working as a producer was even worse. Having to meet and be accountable directly to studio executives and also shepherd writers is not my idea of a good time. It is sort of like mediating between armed gangs of alternately slothful and violent four-year-olds.

The combination of these two unpleasant career avenues left me jangly and raw, even when dealing with Mr. Perfect. Unhappy workers make unhappy fathers. Time for a change.

The change came by pure luck and a little work—a very little work, I am happy to say. Because of my little scenes in *Ferris Bueller's Day Off,* I had become, through some osmotic process, a cult figure among men and women of a certain age. I was sought out as the prototypical teacher, authority figure, dominant but weak father figure. My monotone voice was in high demand. I got to be a recurring character on one of the best shows ever made—*The Wonder Years.* I also got to do a lot of commercials.

Doing commercials, and especially voice-overs, is the best job on the planet by far. It's fun, it's easy, and it pays well—not by Wall Street standards but by most other measures. It allowed me plenty of free time while I was earning a living. Plus, it was completely frictionless. It got me decent, even good, paychecks without putting me into any kind of remorse.

Second, at about the same time, I started to become somewhat sought after as an expert witness in securities cases. I had written a fantastic amount about securities fraud for *Barron's* and other magazines. I had written a book about securities fraud. Now lawyers were calling me to be an expert witness and consultant in securities cases. This kind of work was not even in the same universe of joy as working on commercials. It was hard work, often involving difficult reading, extremely difficult analysis of frauds, and reducing those observations to writing.

On occasion, this work also involved depositions. A deposition is basically a meeting with lawyers from the other side who are free to torture you, make you feel terrible about yourself, and try to make you look like a mass murderer—all in the name of trying to get from you the opinions you are planning to offer at trial. If there is a worse nonmedical experience, I am not at all sure what it might be. Maybe a Moscow show trial in 1937 with Vishinsky as prosecutor could compete with a deposition.

Still, the depositions did not come up often. And even they, while far more painful than a story meeting at a studio, at least involved some respect for me. I was an "expert witness" after all, not a begging, pleading, wheedling peddler of scripts, which for me is the lowest form of man's existence in Hollywood. Even if the other side treated me as if I were a Trotskyite and they were Beria's henchmen, my side treated me with respect. I was someone important to my side. The exact opposite applies to the work of a scriptwriter, who is often considered a burden and a pest by the very people who hired him.

Plus, reading prospectuses and SEC filings was often interesting, invariably stimulating mentally, and—when done in the name of the stockholders, as I usually did it—socially redemptive. The same can rarely be said about scriptwriting.

The best part of my career changes, though, was that I had far more time to spend with my Tommy Boy. Plus, the time I did have to spend with him was not spent with my guts churning inside out and the blood flowing the wrong way in my veins because I was doing work I hated for people I hated. I could leave a morning's work in the studio feeling like a prince. I left a morning's work in the law library feeling as if I were at least a yeoman, not a low form of political prisoner compelled to do work against my will for a country I hated.

A pleasant, positive frame of mind about one's work is a major contributor to a happier father–son relationship. I got mine by pure luck, but at least I got it. I have no idea how long it will last, but I am grateful for every day that I get to spend not having to do work I hate. It shows in my relationship with Tommy in many ways.

Shortly after I finished the last well-paid screenplay I wrote, about five years ago (I have written a few very small ones since), I went fishing with Tommy at Lake Arrowhead in the surprisingly lofty San Bernardino Mountains. Just before I left, I learned that I had three fine commercials lined up for my return. We were sitting out on a dock and casting our lines into the mountain waters, and I was thinking with the usual dread about what I had to do when I got back in terms of pitch meetings. Then I realized that I did not have to do anything. The commercials would pay the freight. The lake looked calmer. The breeze was fresher. The air was more moist. Tommy could actually sense my calm when I started doing work I liked. "Daddy," he said, "why are you being so good to me?"

"I'm always good to you," I answered.

"But you're really good now. How do I get into commercials?" he asked with his usual blinding insight. He knew what was calming Daddy down.

"It's luck," I said. "Just luck and being there."

"How can I get a job I like?" he asked.

"Well, what would you like?"

"Something that pays a lot and leaves me a lot of time to spend with dogs."

"The best-paying, easiest job is probably financial fraud," I told him.

"Really? What's that?"

"Telling people lies and getting their money away from them and not paying it back. That pays really, really well."

"That sounds great," Tommy said with a big smile. "Is that really a good job?"

"No, not really," I said. "I was kidding."

"What, then?"

"I don't know, but we'll work on it. We don't have to do it today. Today is for the lake and the fish."

As I am writing this chronicle about Tommy and me, I am working on a project at Disney. Thanks to my good pal Al Burton, I am employed to be the host and a daily contestant on a new show Disney is developing to be called (if it ever gets on the air) Win Ben Stein's Money. *It is tense and fun and creative, and I love it a lot. It's also the perfect title, because money and I are like matter and anti-matter. Whenever I have any, it seems to flee from me. When possible, I try to encourage it to flee in Tommy's direction. Anyway, this afternoon we had a particularly fierce competition among three former winners of* Jeopardy *and* Debt *versus me. I won, by sheer luck. When I left, I was stoked beyond speaking. I was buzzing with questions and answers.*

I sped over to Hollywood to pick up Tommy at Temple Israel's fourth grade. He was throwing a ball against the wall of the synagogue, enjoying the afternoon with his schoolmates. As usual, he ran over to me and threw himself into my arms, in an effort to knock me down and also as a try at making sure I picked him up. "Tommy," I said, "I've just been rehearsing for Win Ben Stein's Money.*"*

"At Disney, Daddy?"

"Exactly, my boy," I said, "and now we're going to play for real money. Are you ready to play?"

"You bet, Daddy."

"All right then, my boy. For twenty-five dollars, the president of the Confederacy."

He furrowed his little brow, stuck out his tongue, and said, "Uh . . . uhh . . . Jefferson Davis."

"Right. For a further fifty dollars, name eight states of the Confederacy."

He looked serious and said, "Virginia, Texas, Maryland . . ."

"Buzzz," I answered. "Not Maryland, my native state; that stayed with the Union. Keep going."

"Uh, Florida, Texas . . ."

I reviewed geography with him and then said, "All right, you missed that. For twenty dollars, the two issues over which the Civil War is generally believed to have been fought."

"Slavery and states' rights," he said.

"Exactly."

We turned to the Second World War. "For twenty-five dollars, the name of the world's first production jet fighter."

"Uh . . . uh . . . Messerschmitt, but I can't think of the model number."

"Two-sixty-two. For that you get fifteen dollars. Name of the decisive battle of North Africa."

"El Alamein."

On we went as we shopped for our dinner at Chalet Gourmet. Tommy had won about two hundred dollars. "This doesn't go for college, does it?" he asked. "I want to be sure I get to spend it right away on toys."

"Of course you do," I said.

"All right. Go ahead."

"For fifty dollars, German anti-aircraft weapon later converted into a formidable anti-tank gun."

"Eighty-eight millimeter cannon," he shot back.

The little military historian and game show contestant demanded a gargantuan remote control car as his winnings. I took him over to buy it at Radio Shack. I did not feel bad that at last some money was leaving me for someone I care about, not for a home remodeling contractor or a specialty store or the usual recipient, the IRS. Tommy studied carefully a large chart about how fast each kind of RC car traveled. "Daddy," he asked, "if a car can go fifteen hundred feet per minute, how many miles per hour is that?"

"Let's figure it out. How many minutes in an hour? How much is sixty times fifteen hundred? How many times does roughly five thousand go into ninety thousand?"

I had to force Tommy to do each calculation or even to follow how I did it. I did not mind. Childhood memories of trying vainly to follow my braino father while he did calculations are still fresh. The point I wanted to make to the little game-playing historian was not exactly how to do the analysis. I wanted to show him that I, his lumbering old Dad, could do the math. I find that Tommy generally believes he can do anything that his Dad can do, only better. If I give him time, he will learn how to do it, if only to compete with me, if only because he believes it's possible if he sees me doing it. A boy who sees his Dad doing something believes it's possible for him to do it, too. That is a big lesson of fathering.

That day Tommy bought a truly monstrous RC car, so big that the remote control device alone took ten AA batteries. We got it home, and I helped install the batteries so they were going the right way. Again, I have no ability at electrical things at all. Sometimes, however, I can read simple instructions. My idea was to teach Tommy that reading the directions pays off handsomely. He did read the instructions, God bless him, and proudly set the ferocious-looking beast of a car on the tile floor my wife had just paid over our life savings for.

The damned machine would not work even when properly loaded. "It doesn't matter, Daddy," Tommy said. "This one is too big, anyway. I want a smaller one. We'll get our money back and you can save that for another toy later on and I'll get the smaller one. It's faster, anyway."

"Fine."

"In the meantime, let's play Scrabble."

I laid out the board, and in about half an hour the little bondit had such a commanding lead that I could not catch up no matter what I did. "It's okay, Daddy," he said magnanimously. "That was mostly luck. What game would you like to play that you're still good at? Or do you want to ask me more of those questions? Whatever you like." He loves to win and gets into a very good mood when he does. I think that's called being human.

"I'll ask you more questions," I said. "This time about American involvement in Vietnam. Are you ready?"

"You bet," he said as he stowed away his Scrabble letters. "I'm ready to Win Ben Stein's Money."

SIX

It is not easy to be a father in Los Angeles, especially in the Hollywood part of Los Angeles. There are no places to ride a bike partly because it's so hilly, partly because the traffic is so dense, and partly because even on the boardwalk by the beach here, which is cement, there are panhandlers and gangs and skate-by shootings.

There are essentially no parks here. What parks there are have often become the homes of masses of homeless, crack dealers, panhandlers, and scary people of assorted stripes. The few parks that do not meet that description are covered every afternoon with extremely serious-looking soccer players, often from non-English-speaking countries, often so physically fit that they can kick the ball with deadly force. Occasionally, one of them kicks a ball near my son, and it scares me.

The beaches are lovely at some times of the year but a beach, by definition, is a barren, treeless place. At the times when they are not mobbed, they are usually also cool and rainy.

There are only a few public places where the father–son relation is not drawn to buying things. That is, the few public places that are safe and not disgusting are usually shopping centers, filled with things that compel Tommy to nag me to buy him those things.

Plus, in L.A. kids are always in some kind of rush, often connected with structure. There are after-school classes—chess, art, science, music, karate (and, by the way, why are kids so obsessed with karate?). Then there is homework. Then there's *The Simpsons,* virtually the only event that will compel my son to run from one room to another of our house. Then there is compulsory reading. On weekends there is cursed soccer (always far too early in the morning) and desperately needed rest after the horribly early soccer. Then there are shopping trips—and more shopping trips. Your kid's friends are always in some damned kind of activity, too, and their mothers and fathers are usually working on something—gainful employment, tax cheating, weight loss, muscle toning, or age (or sex) reversal. Everyone is in a mad hurry.

I have lived in enough cities to know that few are as uncompromisingly anti-family as L.A.; also, few are really father–son friendly. There is little in a city of beauty, peace, or the nature that offers salvation to man's soul. Maybe modern urban life is just not parent–child friendly. Cities are built for commerce, not for riding bikes. Society is about money, after all, at least at the levels of typical urban behavior. The idea that Los Angeles—or any other American city—might be geared to optimize the parent–child experience was apparently not in the plans of city fathers.

Big cities really are about getting and spending and after-school classes, not about hanging around with your son on a dock with your fishing lines in clear water. Or, to put the matter slightly differently, it is great to be a dad anywhere, but it is better in some kind of fantasy setting of a small town set in an outcropping of the Rocky Mountains. That idea had been going through my mind for a while when something happened in the summer of 1992 to further cement the ties that bind Tommy and me.

The history of that event starts with a commercial director and producer named Mark Story. He used me in many commercials: for Western Union, U.S. West, Dr. Pepper, Twin Valu ShopKo, Nikon, Pan Am, and others. We often talked between takes. He was extremely interested in the stock market, as I was, and loved to talk about the economy. He told me that he owned, among many other possessions, a fabulous home on a hill overlooking Lake Pend Oreille—a place I had never even heard of—in North Idaho. He said it was paradise (except for a neighbor who had shot one of Mark's dogs). He said my life was incomplete unless I spent time in North Idaho. He told me it had a kind of rural peace that I would not find elsewhere. The racists and Nazis that you read about in the papers and see on TV were a hoax, he said, but I could only find out all of that if I went there myself.

So one summer day in 1992, I flew up to Spokane, Washington. Filled with fear of storm troopers, I headed off in a rented car to Sandpoint, Idaho (population, five thousand), the closest town to Mark Story's house. Sandpoint was a revelation. It was on a huge lake ringed with mountains. It had a lovely sandy beach where families played without any amplified noise. The locals were extremely friendly and respectful. God bless the kids, many of them recognized me from TV and clustered around me. There was an adorable main street with sidewalks and friendly stores. The streets of the town were flat to gently hilly, with modest homes and many small churches. Mark Story's home was overwhelming, mighty, too much for me to think about for long, but Sandpoint, in what had been falsely billed as white supremacist territory, was a little jewel of welcome.

Most of all, there was Mark Story's caretaker and home builder, a weather-beaten, rugged fellow named Peter Feierabend, a former high school swimming mate of Mark's. He showed me around, laughed affectionately at the pomp and glory of Mark's home, and then took me on a tour of the lake. He told me how it had been created by a mighty flood caused by the breakup of giant glaciers covering what became Montana and parts of Wyoming. The resultant gouge made Lake Pend Oreille and much of the Columbia River, and then the vast sea of ice flowed out to the Pacific Ocean. There was mighty Indian lore about this event, even though it probably happened before the Indians came to Idaho. Peter loved books and bought me one, called *A River Runs Through It,* about the Montana region near North Idaho. He assured me that I was welcome in North Idaho any time I chose and that I would be under his protection and tutelage.

A few months later, I came back with Tommy. We went to a high school football game, where I was mobbed by autograph seekers (one of them offered to be a babysitter for Tommy). Peter introduced his children: Rachel, six years older than Tommy, and Alex, a mere three years older. Tommy loves the company of older boys, and Alex, then eight, seemed like a god to him. They hit it off magically, wrestling in the autumn leaves on the wide, grassy lawn next to the sandy beach of Lake Pend Oreille.

Later that afternoon, four of us—Peter, Alex, Tommy, and I—walked around town, then drove down to see the Clark Fork of the Columbia River. Soon Tommy and I had that perfect little town where boys and their dads could live in a haze of small town fantasy turned real. Sandpoint was the real McCoy, not an Aspen or a Vail, pretend small towns for the rich, where I would once again feel as if the power players were looking down at me. Sandpoint was a genuine small town with all of the good and bad parts of small town life. Since I was not compelled to earn my living there, I had little of the bad parts, which mostly had to do with low-paying jobs.

The real pull of the place, for reasons that will become overwhelmingly clear, is worth noting again: It was not only its spectacular scenery and the easygoing, safe lifestyle. Yes, it was great that here was a place where Tommy could walk into town from our motel at the age of six and buy candy and toys with his pals. Certainly it was wonderful that he could stroll through the park next to the sandy beach. But Peter Feierabend himself was the true star attraction. Peter was a hippie woodworker-artisan. He was also a caretaker of Mark Story's palazzo. But mostly he hung out with his kids. He took them to school, picked them up, played with them, read to them, and taught them how to ski and sail and fish and mountain-bike. More than anyone since the days of Ozzie Nelson, he was Mr. All-American Dad. If his son wanted a toy gun, Peter would take a piece of cedar and make a toy gun on his band saw. If his daughter wanted an accessory to put next to her bed, Peter would take out his tools and wood and make a puzzle that was not just a visual conundrum but a work of art as a bedside artwork.

Peter shared this genius and this talent with Tommy and me. He took Tommy to the beaver pond next to his house one day on our first visit. "Have you ever caught a fish?" Peter asked.

"No," Tommy said. "I want to catch a fish."

"Well, we'll go out on this raft on my pond and catch a fish," Peter announced.

"Surely you mean you'll try to catch a fish," I interjected. "I mean you can't be sure you'll catch a fish on any given day, can you?" This was my city boy know-it-all ignorance and timidity at work as usual.

"No, I mean we'll catch a fish," Peter said. With that, he and Tommy went out on the pond. They hung two lines over the edge and in about thirty seconds Tommy had his first fish—a tiny little rainbow trout, the first of many he would catch there and throw back.

Tommy had never been on a catamaran. Peter took us out on the lake on his speedy craft. When a high wind came over the lake from the direction of the railroad bridge, Peter guided the tiller and the sail, and the craft flew from City Beach to Contest Point, with Tommy and me hanging on for dear life and Tommy shrieking with joy.

While I always warned Tommy not to jump on me without warning (so that he wouldn't harm my old back or neck), Peter, the strong woodworker, would absorb Alex's and Tommy's sneak attacks, twirl them around, throw them up in the air, and catch them. "I've got you, you sack of potatoes," he would say. "I've got you now."

Then Peter took us to the dock of Keith Sheckler's Windbag Marina and showed Tommy how to attach a lure to a line, tie it securely, and cast it onto the water. He taught Tommy how to thread the line through the guides on the pole and even how to untangle the line when it got caught in the spinner.

One day we all, fathers and sons, piled into my rented Oldsmobile and drove into British Columbia, up the Kootenai River to Kootenai Bay, and then across the bay on the longest free ferry ride in North America. The weather was cold and raw, but Tommy and Alex stood out on the deck looking at the water, the eagles, and the ospreys. Meanwhile, Peter and I had soup in the dining room. When the ferry reached the other side of the bay, Peter took Tommy to a fishing goods shop to buy tackle and lures. The whole way back, they talked about fishing and Peter explained how to pick a certain lure for a certain fish.

The beauty of this, or part of the beauty, was that when Peter showed these things to Tommy, he also showed them to me. Then he would say to Tommy, "Next time, your Dad will help you do that." Peter would show me how, watch me do it, and say, "Your fingers aren't used to doing anything very complicated but they'll get used to it and then Tommy will learn and then we'll teach someone else to fish." Sure enough—amazingly—the next time I would be able to help Tommy untangle the line or reset the spinner or I would have at least a vague inkling about what kind of bait to use for what kind of fish.

Tommy, Alex, Peter, and I would have dinner frequently at a local place called Connie's, where loggers gathered to drink coffee and smoke cigarettes. Peter would give the boys a detailed description of how to make, say, a wooden glider. Then Peter would ask me about some aspect of Hollywood or political life. When Tommy interrupted, Peter would say, "Listen to your father, Tommy. He's talking about things that are a lot more important than building a glider."

Probably Peter was Tommy's first idol. Certainly he was the first idol to tell him that his old dad was worth listening to and respecting even if he did not know how to operate a band saw or guide a catamaran. Tommy picked it up and followed the lead: He listened more closely and paid more attention after spending time with Peter and me.

Peter was also extremely confident in his belief that I could handle the boys when he was working or having a hypoglycemic attack, a painful, disorienting condition to which he was frequently subject because of his acute diabetes. For example, when he could not take the boys skiing, he just told me I should do it and assumed I could. Even though I fell down constantly during our first outing, fairly soon I could indeed take the boys skiing. Peter assumed I could take them fishing—I who hated to even touch a live fish—and soon I did that, too.

Best of all, Peter assumed I could discipline Tommy and Alex, and then another boy or two, and assured me that just the mantle of "Dad," confidently borne, carried all the authority I needed to control the boys. Amazingly, he was right. I found that if I just spoke sharply to them in about the same tone Peter would use, they would pay attention to me. Or I could just tell them what we were going to do, not have any argument about it (say, miniature golf instead of go-karts), and the boys would follow my lead. Peter was like a lovable but unchallengeable drill instructor. He lined up the recruits—Tommy and Alex—and told them that Sergeant Ben was now running the show and they had better listen up—and they did.

This fellow whom I met by the merest chance, a caretaker, had the view that boys will be boys; that they will always be recalcitrant, lazy, self-obsessed, and superwasteful; and that they were just evolving into young men, which would be even worse. Peter had a number of memorable epigrams about little boys. For example, he said that one boy would do the work of one boy, two boys together would do the work of half a boy, and three boys would get no work done at all. *"Boy,"* he often said, "is a synonym for *waster of time and money.*" (This totally confirmed my own beliefs on the subject.) Peter saw boys as highly flawed, lazy, undisciplined creatures and believed that it was the father's natural job to be the boss and that fathers could not expect boys to be responsible, sensible, or altruistic—that was why they were called boys. But Peter loved his boy and my boy and was most truly alive when he was around them.

Peter also believed that a boy should be not only respectful but affectionate towards his father. Peter was extremely physical with Alex. He often picked him up, hugged him spontaneously, often with no clear reason, and the boy responded enthusiastically. Alex was by far the most affectionate little boy to his dad that I had ever seen. His example has encouraged Tommy to actually hug me without being bribed to do so (usually a hug is a means of getting a toy, but sometimes it happens on its own). Tommy is far more physical and affectionate to me than most of the other boys I see, and this comes from my following Peter's example and Tommy following Alex's example.

Above all, the boys had to know who was calling the shots. And they had better get used to it. With that attitude even a little bit in evidence, they did get used to it. More to the point, by watching the interaction between Peter and his son, Tommy got used to the idea that I, Daddy, naturally called the tune.

Following in Peter's footsteps was a major instiller of self-confidence for me. More, it was a giant step towards offering both Tommy and me a model of father–son behavior. When in doubt, I would think, *Well, how would Peter do it?* and usually whatever came to mind was the right answer. Peter was in most ways the platonic ideal of a Dad, the wilderness-loving, hippie–philosopher Dad whom boys naturally respect. Just by being around him, I picked up more of it than I ever thought I would. With a Feierabend-style confidence, I was on my way to being a part-time, small-town nerd-dad. Peter's role as a hippie Ozzie Nelson worked well for all of us. For example, not long after watching other people seeming to have a great time on the lake with their powerboats, I decided it was time for Tommy and me to have a boat. In fact, two boats.

One cool day in early fall, Peter, his son, Tommy, and I went over to a marina in the tiny hamlet of Hope, Idaho (former home of the artist Ed Kienholz), and looked at boats. A goofy salesman showed us a fifteen-year-old Sea-Ray that looked nice (it even had a head) and it was ready for a test drive. The lake was deserted and smooth. The salesman started it up and off we went away from the shore. In about sixty seconds, smoke started to billow from the engine compartment. Then a rubbery burning smell. Then sparks. The salesman turned off the engine as little flames licked around it. It would not restart (we did not really want it to). The radio did not work. We had no cell phone. Despite the salesman's earlier assurances, the boat had no fire extinguisher or life jackets. The wind was starting to blow, and it was getting dark. I knew that somewhere to the west there was an immense and terrifying dam at Albeni Falls. We could go over it like Humphrey Bogart and Katharine Hepburn in *The African Queen*. I was scared. In fact, I was frantic.

Meanwhile, Peter was sitting calmly on a seat in the fantail of the boat and smoking a cigarette. "What are we going to do?" I wailed. "I don't want to fall over that dam."

Peter blew out a long trail of smoke and laughed. "The dam is about thirty miles away. We might be drifting two miles an hour. We're not in any danger."

"But it'll be dark soon," I said. "Then what?"

"Somebody will come by," he said. "Sheriff or somebody."

In about a half hour, we drifted by a private isle named Warren Island. We could see two workmen working on a house on a hillside. "I know them," Peter said. "That guy is David Braun, a beekeeper and a contractor. I'll call him." Then, in a staggeringly loud voice, Peter shouted out, "David. It's Peter Feierabend. Our boat's broken. Come get us."

After a few more *hallos* of that kind, I saw a man head down to the dock, get in a work boat (a sort of motorized flatboat), and head our way. "See," Peter said. "That wasn't so bad. Nobody drowned. Nobody went hungry."

We were towed back to port, and then—after many effusive thanks from me to David Braun and many scowls at the boat salesman—we headed back in darkness to Sandpoint. "There's a lesson here," Peter said. "Make good decisions and plan. From now on, always have a cell phone if you feel afraid on the water. Always have lots of life jackets. Always have a fire extinguisher. You just learned some good things today for almost nothing."

I had learned some good lessons about fathers and sons, too. Tommy stayed calm through the entire ordeal and treated it as an adventure. So did Peter's son. I was the only one who was terrified. I learned that if the main leader in a group of fathers and sons stays calm, the kids stay calm. I learned that preparation is priceless. Above all, I saw that Peter saved us; that the lake, with friends all around, was nowhere near as dangerous as I had feared; and that, after some training and with more confidence, the lake would be wide open for Tommy and me.

The next summer, 1995, Tommy and I bought two boats: a small one, basically a rowboat with a small outboard engine, for him and a twenty-foot motorboat for me. In no time at all, Peter, the boys, and I were hurtling up and down the lake from Bottle Bay to Whiskey Rock, from Hope to the Green Monarchs, without a serious mishap of any kind. Soon I was taking the boat out on the lake with me as skipper, Alex mooring us, and Tommy occasionally helping to steer.

The boat became a magnet for Tommy's pals in Sandpoint. Four or five boys and girls would clamber aboard and off we'd go, usually to a point near Garfield Bay. There the kids would jump off the stern into the freezing water (it seemed freezing to me) and swim around, laughing and screaming, then jump up on the boat and do cannonballs on top of each other. Just as Peter Feierabend had predicted, the boys and girls followed my orders if I gave them with sufficient assurance and directness. It was almost as if they were programmed to follow my lead. I tried, again taking Peter's example, never to show fear or concern on the lake, and, indeed, there rarely was cause for concern (I also had dozens of life jackets, a fire extinguisher, a phone, another phone, a whistle, an air horn, and food on hand at all times).

A boat, especially a fiberglass craft like my Thompson, is in some ways a lot like a father–son duo. The boat can take a lot of dings: You can hit a dock too hard, go the wrong angle across wake, gun it a few times with the outboard gear trimmed higher than it should be. The boat will still work and carry you around if you do not go too far out of bounds. What the boat mostly wants is to be active, to be used, to go somewhere. If it's used a lot, it's happy. Or at least so it seems to an anthropomorphic city boy like me.

The relationship of a late-forties man to a group of small children in a boat is a little like the relation of Captain John Paul Jones to the sailors on the *Bon Homme Richard.* The kids just assume you know what you're doing. The boat in some dumb but still meaningful way knows who's the boss. And the lake likes company. So once I had that boat out on Lake Pend Oreille with my son and his pals, I was all set.

I like to think that Tommy also derived some status from the fact that the boat the kids were on belonged to his dad. Tommy was always the most junior member of his team of friends. They always let him know it, in the manner of small children. But Tommy was not defenseless. In going from at first saying, "You can't drop me head first off the boat because it's my dad's boat," to saying, later in the summer, "You can't lock me in the cabin because it's *our* boat," he was showing that our experiences were giving him some feeling of command out on the lake. The other kids had boats, too, by and large, but we spent the most time on our boat because I was not at work. Tommy got to be the junior commodore, and for a little boy to feel jointly in command of a boat is not a bad feeling for him to have. Anything that teaches a child responsibility is worth its weight in gold. Of course, I also derived status from being the Admiral for all of these small adventurers and pirates. Tommy's dad had the boat. Tommy and his dad were the centers of that tiny world. As for captaining your child and his pals on an enormous, almost empty lake on a cloudless summer day: Nice work if you can get it.

We came to Sandpoint in the winter, too. For me, the skiing was always a chore. I do not like falling on skis and having a horrible time getting up. But in the flatland, in the town itself, winter was a delight. Snow is a basic building block of the sense of wonder. In Sandpoint we got plenty. The first time it snowed at night, Tommy, Alex, Peter, and I headed across town from the Edgewater Hotel to The Hydra Restaurant. We passed by subtly molded and hewn lawn lamps that Peter Feierabend had made with his hands in his workshop, now covered with gauzy white snow. We went under the snowfall as it poured down by the city lights. Tommy and

Alex ran ahead in the snow and were joined by other boys. In Sandpoint, little boys travel in packs. The boys made snowballs and tossed them at each other with indifferent results. Every so often Alex, who was bigger than Tommy, would pack together a truly immense snowball and gesticulate menacingly towards him. Tommy would run to me, hide behind me, and say, "You can't hit me. *When I'm touching Daddy, it's a safe zone.*" It is magic every time I hear him say that.

On other snowy nights, when Peter had to work on his lumber for his docks, Tommy and I would set out across town on our own. There are some nights of fatherhood that cannot be explained, only described. One was the first night Tommy and I marched through the snow of Sandpoint down deserted sidewalks, with the snow making a white halo behind the street lamps. We made our way across the bridge over Sand Creek, along First Street, past the Elks and the Eagles, past the closed-down candy store, past the Sandpoint Bagel Shop, and past the loggers eating at the counter at Connie's. Tommy was six. He would hold my hand for a minute, then run on ahead, make snowballs, and throw them at me. I would occasionally scoop up snow and throw one back. Tommy hid behind trees, behind cars in the used car lot, in alleys, and then came out and bombarded me with his white snowy missiles. After a while he got tired, and walked as he leaned on me and asked me to wrap him inside my jacket. By the time we got to the Safeway and then the Gas-n-Go for lottery tickets, we were both intoxicated from the cold and the beauty and from having ourselves to ourselves in the snow. I think that was the best walk I have ever taken in my life. I felt as if I had entered one of those small glass balls where a snowstorm arises when you shake them and that Tommy and I would live forever inside this globe, throwing snowballs at each other under the street lamps of a small North Idaho town. Some days of fatherhood are too magical to be explained.

One day in the fall of 1996, two of Tommy's pals from Sandpoint came to visit us in California. I took them out to our house in Malibu, and they settled themselves in front of the Nintendo 64. They quarreled about whose turn it was, yelled at each other, maneuvered some little guy named Mario for hours, and then fell asleep.

In the morning they awakened before I did. I could hear one of them, a wiry young fellow named Jeb, saying that they had to "explore." They scrambled up and down the heavily wooded hill next to our house and played near the base of an immense tree in a "fort" Tommy had built from leftover lumber. After racing their remote control cars back and forth in the driveway, they discovered a big box of fireworks that a reader in Alabama had sent to me about a year before. "Wow!" said one of Tommy's pals from Idaho. "Wow! Let's shoot off those Roman candles. Let's do it now before your dad wakes up."

"No way," said Tommy Stein. "This is a fire hazard area. No way." I could hear them talking as I lay in bed with the dog.

"Well, then why do you even have them if this is a fire hazard area and you can't set them off? Do you just keep them in a box or what?" asked one of his little provocateur pals.

"No," Tommy said with perfect aplomb, "I set them off when my daddy supervises, 'cause he's been setting off fireworks all his life and he really knows how to do it so it's really cool and also so it's safe."

"Well, can you wake him up, so he can do it right now?" asked Jeb.

"No, 'cause my daddy has to do really important things for the Republicans later today," I could hear Tommy say. "So he has to rest."

"I bet he just lights them the same as everybody else," Jeb said. "I mean, he's an actor. *What does he know about fireworks?"*

"Oh, yeah?" Tommy asked with confident defiance. "Look at this. This is a snake hole. My dad put a Roman candle down this hole a few days ago and then put this cinder block on top of it and then it exploded and I'll bet a whole family of rattlesnakes was killed. And my dad did that. So he knows all about fireworks, so, poo."

Even half asleep, I sighed and drew a deep satisfying breath. Praise from Caesar is praise indeed.

Later that week, after his pals had returned to Idaho, Tommy and I went to the final event of the desperate Dole–Kemp '96 campaign. It was a rally on the grounds of beloved Pepperdine University, with Kemp as the star and yours truly as master of ceremonies. Tommy met the local Republican cast of characters and then sat watching them, under the gaze of his caretaker, Tina. When the event was over, Jack Kemp—as was his custom—tossed dozens of little rubber footballs into the crowd. I tried to get him to throw one to Tommy, but my son was too far back and too small to catch one. I dug one out of the Dole–Kemp campaign box for Tommy.

As the crowd melted away, I walked across the green hillside, with Tommy hanging on my arm. "Daddy," Tommy said, "why don't you run for something?"

"I don't want to, my boy. I hate committee meetings. Plus, I don't want nosy people prying into my life."

"Why not?"

"Because I've done stuff I'm not proud of, and I don't want people snooping into it and writing about it."

"Yeah, but you've also done a lot of good stuff. Like, you teach me all about the Civil War and put me to bed and teach me about the presidents."

"That's my job," I said.

At the end of the day, when the Republican debacle had become clearer and the dancing and smiling and lip biting from Arkansas had become unbearable to a Dole fan like me, I sat in the dark of Tommy's room. He was listening to an audiotaped book about the use of Bikini atoll as a testing place for nuclear bombs. After a few moments, without saying a word, he stretched out his little hand and took my index finger. "You did a good job at that rally," Tommy said. "You should run for something," he suggested again.

"That would take me away from you too much, my boy," I said.

"No. I would run with you and you would home-school me. We'd fly all around going to rallies. And Mommy would meet us and bring us money and clean clothes. It would be cool."

Then he turned over, sighed, and closed his eyes. He fell asleep holding my finger. I hope Bill Clinton had as good a night as I did.

SEVEN

It would be easy, but it would be wrong, to say that once I had the seal of approval of Peter Feierabend and once Tommy and I had strolled the streets of Sandpoint, Idaho, by snowy moonlight, our lives flowed smoothly on into paradise. I wish I could say that once I reached the stage where Tommy automatically expected to spend time with me and looked forward to it, life was easy and free.

True, by the time Tommy was in third grade, he looked ecstatic when I came to get him at school. He simply flew into my arms and wanted me to take him all around town—mostly to McDonald's, 7-Eleven, and KayBee Toys—every afternoon. And as you might predict, his behavior in school was spectacularly improved once he spent a lot of time with his dad. It's not just coincidence that children with fathers who are paying good attention (i.e., not beating them for the hell of it) have far better records in school, in human relations, and in work than children who lack this attention.

A certain male energy apparently comes off fathers, and kids often seem to require it in order to develop. In fact, it's clear to me that even grown-ups need male energy to develop and feel secure. (I notice that restaurants staffed entirely without men seem to run chaotically.) This is my own feeling and probably violates many canons of political correctness. *Eppur si muove.* Nevertheless, it's true. There is much to be said for female energy. I have spent an insane amount of my life chasing after it. But strong male energy (such as I witnessed in Peter Feierabend) has a soothing, calming quality that kids need. Or maybe I should retreat to the unassailable fortress of personal experience and personal reaction and say that I know that I needed it and that my son needs it.

Without male energy, Tommy was a menace and a disruptive force in class. With it, he is a wise guy and a prankster but a constructive member of his little group at school and in soccer (yuck) and among his pals in North Idaho. Without it, he cried and threw terrible tantrums. He felt fragile and was easily cast into wild, defensive confusion. He lacked some kind of solid center that children who have male energy around them seem to have. (I guess I'll get yelled at for this.) With it, he can laugh more easily and stay calmer. He can also make friends more easily. Tommy stands up for himself amazingly well when he knows I am nearby or can be summoned. (I am in awe of how strongly he resists being pushed around even by kids much older than he is. I hope it has to do in part with his sure knowledge that his dad is right behind him.) He is much closer to being a whole person now that he has male energy around him—even if that male energy, though often extremely tired, is just lying in bed reading *The Wall Street Journal* while he watches *The Simpsons.*

However, this is far from the end of what needs to be done with Tommy Stein and for Tommy Stein or with and for Ben Stein. Life is all process and so is raising Tommy Stein. For one thing, Tommy Stein is the little boy of two older parents, who are both madly in love with him. Because we have been in the labor force for a longer time than most parents of nine-year-olds, we are in a position to buy him almost any toy he craves. We know how much he enjoys toys. We live to see him smile, and thus we are hardly ever able to deny him any toy he asks for on a repeated basis. If the kids of America all had parents like us, Nintendo would be bigger than General Motors. Besides, there are the potent economic arguments for indulging Tommy: If we spend fifty dollars on him now, he enjoys it for at least a day and sometimes for weeks. When he is fifty-two, that fifty dollars—even that fifty dollars compounded so that it's a thousand dollars—will mean little to him (by then a thousand dollars will buy a barely passable meal). Plus, if we buy him something he greatly enjoys right now, he gets the pleasure of it straight into the vein, as one might say. There is no problem about estate taxation, probate, or trustees. That money is going to make him laugh and feel good right now without Uncle Sam or lawyers cutting off any part of it. Not to mention that it makes us feel incredibly good to see him feel good. And again, it's out of our estate, so it cannot be confiscated when we die under the government's astoundingly aggressive death taxation program.

That is, all of us benefit a lot from a small expenditure now *and* avoid the dead hand of the IRS coming between our labor and our enjoyment.

The argument for spending time with Tommy is even more direct and clearer: If we spend a day with him, it's a pure gift to him, to us, to his future. We did not work on that day and thus have no taxes to pay on it, so again we cut the IRS out of it. And we get that unique strength into him that comes from time with Mom and Dad. If we worked and left him money, we would deprive him of pleasure and strength here and now, deprive ourselves of pleasure with him in the here and now, and leave a juicy target for the revenooers in years to come. Time invested directly in our kids cuts out all middlemen, all possibility of foreshortening, and gets directly to the desired result—a stronger, happier kid. Why men and women spend their children's whole lives chained to a desk or in thrall to a job, just so the kid (who never knew the parents) can watch the IRS take away the money they slaved for, is a mystery to me. Time with the kid is the key ingredient in childrearing. Time spent at work, even to produce income, is a decidedly second-best scenario. If I repeat this, it's because it's important. Children are not one of the end products of work. Children are the goal all by themselves, and work is largely a distraction from that goal.

My wife and I realize that while the economic argument for spoiling Tommy is strong, there may also be an argument against spoiling him. We just want to make the point that there are arguments for buying him toys now instead of having the money pass into a trust he will get when he's fifty—if Uncle Sam is in a forgiving mood.

As for methods of discipline, neither of us parents has the stomach to strike Tommy except under truly exceptional circumstances. In his whole life, he has only been spanked a few times. The last time I hit him was a trivial bop on the head with a small bag of Milano cookies that made him pretend to cower, laugh, and demand a new bag of cookies. In other words, he is not physically disciplined to any substantial extent, although he does remember that I have spanked him in the past, and when I get very angry at him and look like I might spank him, he responds with some modicum of obedience.

In fact, those few spankings and the memories they inspire are almost the only means I have of disciplining

Tommy besides bribery, which is not really discipline. It does not bother him to be sent to his room. After all, he has a mountain of toys to play with in his room. He has a truck filled with little kids' books and Star Wars books and Jurassic Park books to read in his room. He does not seriously care about being barred from watching TV for a day, or even a week. He knows he is always allowed to be with me when I am watching TV. And he knows that when Alex and I go out, he can always charm the babysitter and sneak in some TV watching. He does hate like the devil to be kept from playing his vile video games, though. Threats of withholding them are taken seriously indeed, but once they are withheld for a day or two, Tommy becomes inured to their absence. Further threats to keep them from him mean little. He is modestly afraid of being kept from playing with his friends, especially his best friend, Alex, but even that does not frighten him for long—because I want so badly for him to have friends and be with them that I rarely can make myself keep him away from playtime with them.

Raising my voice to my son and yelling at him until his spirit is broken is not an option. I had it done to me when I was a child. I did not like it, and I will never do it to him. I do not want his spirit broken under any circumstance.

When I was a small child and up until junior high, my mother consciously sought to remold my personality and make me into someone else—namely, someone who would, as she often said, apply the seat of his pants to the seat of a chair and study, study, study without resistance. Her ideal little boy was, in part, one who would come home from school, sit down, study until dinner, and then study until he fell asleep. Then that little boy would come home every six weeks with the best grades in his class. The other part of her ideal little boy would be tough—a *shtarker,* as we Jews say—and would not run from any conflict—except to the extent that this conflicted with his role as a student. He would not be frightened or emotional but would phlegmatically and bravely and uncomplainingly move forward through life.

My mother's ideal for me—at least at a certain time of my life—was a combination of Yeshiva *bucher,* bond trader, and New York State motorcycle cop. How she formed this combination of models is not entirely impossible to see: In the old country, and even in America, Jews got ahead and made their way if they did well in school. They also made their way if they were tough. Her father was legendarily tough. She endlessly recounted how when he had to have a tooth pulled, he would refuse ether, stand up after the extraction, shake hands with the dentist, and leave the room to return to his business. Where the worship of New York State motorcycle cops came from, I have no idea at all, except to suspect that they must have cut a dashing figure to her when she was a small child in Monticello, New York.

Whatever the reasons for my mother's wishes about how to mold me—and I am sure they were well intentioned—the effect on me was disastrous. I was not by nature or nurture or God's plan the kind of boy my mother wanted me to be. I loved to read, but not compulsorily. I loved to think and analyze but, again, not on schedule. Most of all, I disliked being shut up indoors for any reason at all. The life of the Yeshiva *bucher* sitting on a bench in his *cheder* and memorizing Mishnah seemed then and seems to me now a dreary life indeed. I liked to learn but not at the point of the lash and not in competition with anyone else.

I was also the farthest thing from a *shtarker.* I was alternately shy and playful, but never tough. At no time have I been a shrewd cardplayer or gambler or negotiator or litigator. My natural inclination is to either lie in bed and read or play outside. My mother's plans for me simply were not me.

One of my major goals in life is to avoid doing anything even remotely like that to Tommy. I want him to have a general idea of what acceptable behavior is—doing his homework, being respectful to his elders and friends and teachers—but to have maximum leeway within that large, roomy structure to be who he is. This means I do not yell at him (except under the direst circumstances), try to break his spirit, or try to make him into something he's not. I do not see him as a computer to be programmed. He is a human being built to work and struggle but also to exult in life itself. He has been programmed largely by God at conception, and I want to shape that to a productive, law-abiding form, but not at the cost of making him wonder who he is and bite back against himself whenever he starts to feel happy and proud of himself. All of the sacrifices of every prior Stein generation are meaningless if Tommy cannot take a good swig of enjoyment from life's glass.

Tommy is innately wonderfully lively, inventive, and full of the "spirit of play," as he always puts it. He can take the most ordinary materials and invent a game or create a decoration. I constantly find little crepe paper flowers, clay figures of dogs and cats, and drawings of space ships all around the house. From the age of about five, Tommy could dress up his dog, Susie, in inventive ways—for example, as a clown, a bat, a cowdog. Tommy can create vast cities on his computer. He makes up stories about life in outer space and has done so since he was seven. I do not want to spoil the spirit that came to him from genetics or nurture or imitation of Mommy or me—or imitation of Ren and Stimpy. I do not want to throw around my weight to make my son into something he is not. Maybe my way will not work either, but I notice that Tommy seems to have about as much joy in a single afternoon as I had in my entire childhood. He may be spoiled, but he is also amazingly happy and high-spirited. In other words, so far so good on our lax upbringing: Tommy is creative and, above all, capable of complete, unself-conscious enjoyment (a first for a young Stein of any generation). He is, however, as might be predicted, a fantastically lazy child—although maybe not by modern middle-class American standards.

A buck-passing possible causal connection with Tommy's sloth is that since he was born, he has had a caregiver attached to him in addition to his old ma and pa. The first one was a superstrict baby nurse who got him on an admirable schedule. For seven years after that, he had an older woman of Mexican origin, Elena, as his caregiver and nanny. This woman, a totally devoted soul, followed him from room to room picking up after him and cooking for him and generally doing for him what Alexander the Great's body servants might have done for him or what an aide-de-camp might have done for the Supreme Allied Commander, Europe after the Supreme Allied Commander had completed the triumphant landing in France. When Tommy was just out of diapers, I once found Elena standing next to him at the toilet to wipe off his penis in case he dripped after he peed. Tommy could yell for Elena from anywhere in the house to bring him anything, and it was there as fast as her old legs could carry her. No matter how many times we pleaded with her or ordered her to stop catering to him so lavishly, she kept on treating him like a young Middle Eastern potentate. Tommy was her god.

However, this fact of the ultradevoted child-care giver without the will or inclination to restrain or command inhibits discipline, to put it gently. It also attacks self-reliance. In addition to our restraint in using physical punishment and our refusal to yell at or to seriously deprive our son, Elena's total servitude toward him did not help his attitude. In other words, Tommy is a classic child of our age, that is, a classic child of parents like us in our age. Maybe worse than classic.

It is stunning to me every time he does it, but when Tommy prepares for bed, he often just leaves his shoes, socks, and clothes where he happened to be standing when he took them off. No matter how many times I make him get out of bed to retrieve his clothes and put them in the hamper, he does it again, that is, leaves his clothes on the floor of the living room or kitchen. He is far too old for that, and I hate it.

It terrifies me that Tommy can leave a remote control car that's as big as a red wagon in a darkened hallway at the top of the stairs leading to the basement. But Tommy Stein does it over and over again.

The worst, most maddening, aspect of Tommy's laziness has to do with his homework. For years he resisted doing it by any means necessary. For a subject he truly hated—Hebrew, for example—he simply did not bring home his assignment. Even if I asked him if he had his homework assignment when I picked him up at school, he would prevaricate. When I tracked down the assignment from another parent, Tommy would cry and sulk and pretend to be ill to avoid doing it. The variety of health-related excuses Tommy invented for failing to do his homework would make Ferris Bueller blush. He actually spits on his hands and wipes them on his forehead to simulate the damp, warm feeling of fever. He pretends to pass out at the table while he is doing his lessons so as to make us think he is so fatigued that he cannot possibly think. He drops his pencils and papers to make us think he has some kind of palsy. I believe he could have taught Huck Finn a thing or two.

Tommy's handwriting is almost unbelievably poor. You have to see it to believe it. Even to me—and I have been reading it for years—it is close to undecipherable. No matter how many times I tell Tommy to redo, say, an impossible *e* or a ridiculous *g*, he does it again just as poorly. His numbers are often even worse. I love every comma that proceeds from his mouth, but this little maniac's rendering of numbers is infuriating. His articulation is impossible: he is so lazy in his speech that I often cannot make out a word he says in a whole paragraph. Tommy is so lazy that he often does a homework assignment literally without starting to read the instructions. The results are what you would expect.

Thus, we have a spoiled child to a large extent—although we reckon that he is better behaved than most of his peers, and that's something. But how—absent withholding of affection or making threats of physical punishment—do we get him to behave and act responsibly? We try to reason with him, to explain to him why what he is doing is good or bad either for him or for the world around him. This moral suasion sometimes works, but it often does not.

The principle that a nine-year-old should refrain from leaving a light turned on in a room he's not in because it costs money and wastes fuel and pollutes the air might mean something in an earth science textbook. It might mean a lot in a TV sitcom about an environmentally correct family. It only sometimes means something to Tommy Stein. The "sometimes" is usually when the principle is accompanied by a bribe or a threat of no video games. The idea that Tommy Stein should not order food at McDonald's that he is not going to eat because it is wasteful to Mommy and Daddy and breeds carelessness makes sense to profit-maximizing, efficient *homo economicus*. For years it fell on deaf Tommy Stein ears—unless accompanied by a more immediate economic incentive like a promise or delivery of a video game. That is, Tommy is truly economic man, not theoretical economic man.

What else do we do? I lecture Tommy about his laziness constantly. I preach to him and try to explain to him how important schoolwork is. "Tommy, my boy," I say to him, "it's not at all clear that Mommy and Daddy will be able to leave you enough money so you do not have to work for a living. I hope we can, but it's a long shot. Even if we did win the lottery, it would be better psychologically for you to work for a living. It would give you a sense of purpose that you might otherwise lack and need. It would keep you from having long, idle days on which to waste your life."

At this point, he usually interrupts to ask if we can go to Subway for a sandwich.

"When you do enter the workforce," I tell him, "you will have a much better time if you have some education. If you have some special skill, you will be able to get a much higher hourly wage than if you lack some special, valuable skill. The difference is amazing. Mommy gets a couple of hundred dollars an hour, sometimes more, for being a lawyer—indoors, in an air-conditioned office, sitting in a chair, and often just schmoozing on the phone. A construction worker gets maybe ten or fifteen or twenty dollars an hour for very hard, tiring work in dangerous conditions in cold weather or hot weather or sometimes rainy or snowy weather. Quite a difference, eh, my boy?"

At this point, he often asks me, "Daddy, how much does a vehicle designer get per hour?"

"If you are one of the top ones," I reply, "an enormous amount. Maybe thousands of dollars per hour. But the point is that you need education to do any of these things. Plus—and this is at least as important as what you get paid—if you have a good education, you can do far more interesting work than if you don't. You are more likely to do work that uses your mind and creativity than if you lack education. Plus, you are much more likely to be the one who is in charge if you have the education. You're not just a piece of driftwood floating along out there in the sea. Education is the key to everything."

"Yes, but, Daddy, how much does a vehicle designer get paid per hour?"

"Tommy, I don't know exactly, but my point is a little broader than that. It has to do with having something in your brain that makes you valuable. Some kind of knowledge mixed with your own creativity and your ability to get along with others that allows you to have some control over your life and get the good things you want out of life."

"How much do race car drivers get paid?"

"It doesn't matter, because you are never allowed under any circumstances to be a race car driver."

"Why not?"

"Because you are not allowed under any circumstances to do anything that could foreseeably harm you."

"But, Daddy . . ."

"The idea is that you are supposed to do something *safe,* above all, that requires some special skill that will pay you enough to have a decent life and also express yourself. Together with whatever Mommy and Daddy can give you, you might be able to earn enough so that you don't just have to sell your labor and can have your money work for you while you do something that is artistic or serves the common good. We'd like for you to have human capital sufficient to have a good life. That's the bottom line. That means you have to get an education. Education is really cheap. It's really easy, and it changes your life."

"School is not always easy," Tommy often argues. (I am happy to say that I have explained to him enough times what human capital is that he doesn't even have to ask what it is. He knows it's what you have in your head that allows you to make your way in the world.) "Sometimes school is really hard," the little angel says.

"That's true, but it's a lot easier than working. Try working at manual labor or retail sales or driving a truck for a few dollars an hour, and then tell me how it feels to work as compared to studying a book. In life the really hard things have to do with human relationships or health. School, getting an education, is a pretty easy thing by comparison. There's probably nothing that's easier and has a bigger payoff than education. So when we get home, you have to do your homework and pay attention to it as if it meant something to you. *Capisci?*"

Usually, at this point he'll look sullen and pretend that he didn't hear me.

"Tommy, my boy, if you can learn now, when you are a child, to have some responsibility for your work, your whole life will be far easier. If it becomes part of your character to do your work to your best level of ability, to be self-starting and self-motivating when it comes to work, you will be a much happier fellow from now on. Once it gets to be habit, it's easy. If you do not get into the habit of doing your work properly, if you resist learning and doing your work properly, you will find it more difficult year by year. If you manage to fight against doing your work until you get to high school, it will probably be impossible for you to ever recover and catch up. By then, it might well be too late."

At this point Tommy will start to list people who did not have much of an education but who managed to do well in their lives. "But, Daddy, what about Michael Jordan? What about John Travolta? They hardly have any education and look how well they've done. Mommy just wrote up a contract for John Travolta to get paid twenty-two million dollars for one picture. That's a lot more than you get paid."

"Tommy, my boy, it's true that there are a few people who don't have a lot of education who make a good living. Michael Jordan, by the way, does have a pretty good education, and John Travolta is well trained as an actor. But there are millions of people out there trying to be successful actors and athletes. Out of those millions, only a few hundred make a decent living. On the other hand, there are a few million doctors, lawyers, business school grads, journalists, psychologists, and college professors out there, and almost all of them make a decent living and do interesting work and don't have to wait tables while they're waiting for their big break. Yes, there are a few people who make it without education, but to think you're going to be one of them is like thinking you'll win the lottery."

Tommy listens to this, and with a weary sigh he puts himself partly on his chair and lifts up his pencil, as if it weighed a ton, to address his single digit multiplication tables.

I often feel like a nag and a bully when I light into Tommy about this homework thing. For his safety, I try never to do it in a way that frightens him or makes him feel that I won't love him if he doesn't do well in school. But I am really scared of what will happen to him if he continues to be as lazy as he has been thus far. To me he is the angel of the morning. But to the world he could just be another lazy white kid. His mother and I have probably done enough damage by endlessly telling him how much we love him and by coddling him. I think we owe it to him to tell him, as many times as it takes him to learn it, that he will greatly regret it if he does not learn to do his schoolwork.

What is amazing about this struggle is the growth potential of little kids. I started writing this chapter in September of 1996, about the same time I moved back in with Alex and Tommy. Then I got sidetracked by working on *Win Ben Stein's Money*. But from the middle of September 1996 to the middle of January 1997, a sort of sea change came over Mr. Tommy Stein. Little by little, he has become better about his work. Little by little, one painful evening at a time, he has begun to pay attention to what he's doing. His class studied Thailand for a month. Tommy actually threw himself into learning about the monsoons and the Buddha and Chiang Mai and Bangkok. He begged me to take him to Thailand. He actually began reading the newspaper to see if there were any stories in it about Thailand.

I have also been training him to think by asking him arithmetic questions in the car as we drive to Santa Monica or Sandpoint or Malibu. I often promise him a treat if he does them well. I also show him that I can do math fairly well in my head. Wanting to please Daddy, plus seeing that Daddy can do it, has made Tommy into a bit of a math whiz among his pals. When they get together and need to figure out the cost of movie tickets and popcorn, they often turn to Tommy to do the calculation—and he usually does it right. He has started to take some pride in his skill at math. In school he moved from the lowest to the highest level of his class in math. I taught him the formulas for conversion from Fahrenheit to Celsius in a matter of minutes, and he could apply them to show off to his pals in Idaho almost immediately.

Tommy also seems to have actually learned something from his endless watching of TV shows about animals, insects, spiders, and poisonous plants. When we see a spider at our home in Malibu, as we often do, Tommy always knows its name and lethality and other details about it that startle me. He knows a great deal about animals and plants as well. I often question him about them, and he takes some pride in knowing the answers.

He also watches the gory medical operations channel on TV and apparently has absorbed a deal of information about aortas, sutures, plasma, and clamps. He also enjoys watching this material that his Mommy and I are far too squeamish to follow.

Thus, by exhortation, by modest threats, by bribery, and, above all, by example, progress is being made. By some kind of miracle, Tommy has seemingly begun to overcome the inertia of his deep laziness and has begun to do some work. "There are three important lessons in life," I like to tell him, as an echo of my old hippie days. "They are pay attention, pay attention, and pay attention." It may be that moral suasion and exhortation are having some effect on the little angel. He seems to be realizing, with painful slowness, that learning is not his enemy.

Then there is something else that's been motivating Tommy. In about mid-October 1996, we parents at Temple Israel Day School were alerted to an imminent meeting to see if any parents and kids were interested in becoming Cub Scouts and Scout parents. Tommy said he was eager to sign up. I had seen his eagerness for karate (dropped after three weeks), saxophone (dropped after one week, subsequent to our buying a saxophone), and chess lessons (dropped even before the first anniversary of meeting with the tutor). I was not eager to waste more of my good time on his fantasy of the moment.

Naturally, I went to the meeting anyway. Out of the whole school, only a few kids and their bedraggled fathers or mothers showed up. Two neatly dressed Scout leaders in Scout outfits gave a confusing little talk. Tommy could barely be bothered to pay attention. Of course, we signed up anyway.

At the first meeting, though, a certain scouting magic worked on Tommy like Dexedrine. His den mother, a well-organized woman named Kate, showed the boys how to fold the flag. Tommy threw himself into it with startling intensity. Then he watched knot tying and addressed it with similar eagerness. ("Can I learn how to tie a noose? Please?")

He carefully studied the uniform chart and made me take notes, too. I was amazed as I watched it.

A few days later, I returned from a rehearsal of *Win Ben Stein's Money* to first behold Tommy Stein in his Scout uniform. With his hair combed neatly and sporting his new long green pants, matching shirt, natty plaid scarf, and Cub Scout kerchief slide, he looked like a clean-featured, clean-limbed little god. (I often feel as if Tommy really is a god and that when I behold him, I should throw myself on the ground like a primitive before a totem of the deity. I guess this is probably not the proper attitude for a father to have. It shows a certain lack of command.)

At his meetings Tommy behaved with astonishing respect for the den mother. He raised his hand to be recognized before he spoke. He led the Pledge of Allegiance (if you want to have a moving experience, watch your nine-year-old leading the Pledge of Allegiance in a Scout uniform): "Those in uniform, salute. Those not in uniform, hold your right hand over your heart and repeat after me. 'I pledge allegiance to the flag . . . and to the Republic for which it stands . . .'" (He had memorized not just the Cub Scout pledge but much more of his *Webelos Handbook,* including the up-to-the-minute PC requirements for learning how to stop child sex abuse.) At the end of the meeting, Tommy helped to clean up. He folded the flag and taught a newcomer how to do it.

At the third meeting, Tommy was so hipped on the Cub Scout motto that when two fellow Scouts were disorderly in the parking lot of the synagogue, he told them to straighten up and cleaned up after them. Amazingly, after his fourth or fifth meeting, Tommy got down on his hands and knees to pick up crushed bits of popcorn and candy that his fellow Scouts had left on the floor. He was the only boy in the room doing it, and I could not have been happier. At that same meeting, he was awarded his Bobcat Badge. He was the only boy to get it this fast, and he earned it solely because he threw himself into the memorization required and then proudly declaimed what he had memorized before his fellow Scouts.

When he wears his uniform, Tommy is a whole new boy. If he forgets to help me carry in the groceries, I say, "Tommy, didn't you know that a Scout must be helpful?" Without further ado, he helps. If he interrupts Mommy or me at dinner, I say, "Tommy, do you think Scouts are supposed to interrupt their parents at the dinner table?" and he waits (for about five seconds) to speak. After wearing his Scout uniform, he puts it away neatly instead of just leaving it on the floor. Not only that, but Tommy is a far more sociable and social boy when he's in uniform. Wherever we go, he is stopped by present and former Scouts who want to discuss scouting. At a Thai restaurant in West Hollywood, a waiter showed Tommy a photo of himself as an Eagle Scout at a Jamboree in Thailand. At Chalet Gourmet, the rock 'n' roll food store on Sunset, not one but several different shoppers have come up to Tommy to swap salutes and talk about being Webelos or Cub Scouts long ago. By being a Scout, Tommy has become part of an ancient worldwide fraternity. When he talks to these Scouts, he looks them in the face, speaks in whole sentences, and discusses knots and Scout history rather than video game moves.

I am not quite sure why Tommy has pulled himself together so much in his scouting role. Is it structure? Is it the military-style uniform? Is it because I, his old dad, sit there with him through each meeting? Is it some kind of self-selection process that makes him feel elite? Whatever it is, I see him on an upward swing, responding to the good influences around him, and I pray that all of it lasts.

Amazingly, it really seems to be true that Tommy's behavior is improving. He is still a long way away from turning off lights or electric heaters when he leaves rooms. I still find partially eaten food all over his room, and his side of the car is a trash can on wheels. It's often a struggle to make him do his homework. His teachers still note to me a certain insouciance about his duties in class. But he is getting better.

I can already feel the day coming when Tommy is neat and does clean up after himself—and Mommy and I desperately miss the helplessly slobby little boy he was. We are obviously going to have to trade aging for responsibility, and that is not a trade I care to make. Perhaps Tommy picks up this cue from me and acts on it, but I love him as a little boy so much, even as a little Pigpen, that I miss his dirty little socks every time he picks them up. I have a certain foreboding about his teenage years, and a large foreboding about how long I might live after them. In the here and now, everything is under control, and the messy present is at least the present. I know it's my duty to make Tommy neater and better organized. But I know how painful it will be to have a neat house after he leaves for college or wherever he goes, and I can already feel the chill of a house without him.

What follows is a true account of the life of Ben and Tommy Stein in Hollywood in the fall of 1996. On Monday of the week, I was awakened at 8 A.M. by a call from my nutritionist, a former call girl I'll call Buffy. She had spent a difficult weekend with one of her thuggish boyfriends and naturally wanted to take out her sense of victimization on me. She badgered me about my eating, exercise, and lack of respect for colloidal vitamin habits for a half hour and then disappeared off the line as suddenly as she had appeared.

At about noon, I went over to the small Geo Theater in Hollywood, where Disney was staging the "presentation" of Win Ben Stein's Money. *There was no parking anywhere, and it took me, the star of the show, about half an hour to park my car. At the theater we first had run-throughs with contestants who had been* Jeopardy *winners and who were, by and large, far faster on the button than I was and at least as well informed. By the time of the actual event, I was a frazzle of anxiety and fatigue from all those run-throughs.*

The audience was about a hundred men and women who applauded wildly, laughed hysterically, and seemed to appreciate the show as much as I could possibly have hoped. There were only two exceptions: two poker-faced men who sat right in the middle of the audience and stared without expression throughout the show. Naturally, they were the promoters for the show, the top honchos from Disney; they made Buster Keaton look like Marcel Marceau. In the final round I was up against a twenty-five-year-old man with the sides of his head shaved and a slack-jawed, backcountry cracker expression on his face. He beat me devastatingly when I blanked on who the Democratic nominee for vice president in 1984 was (Geraldine Ferraro) and who wrote *I Know Why the Caged Bird Sings* (Maya Angelou).

That day happened to also be my fifty-second birthday. The kind folks from Disney presented me with a fine cake. They sang "Happy Birthday." After most of the people in the show left, I packed my few belongings from my dressing room and put them in the trunk of my car. Tommy, a late arrival at the theater, peered into the trunk and took from it the little blue and white football that Jack Kemp had given us at the rally marking the end of the ill-fated Dole–Kemp campaign a few days earlier at Pepperdine. "Daddy," he said, "let's throw the football here in the parking lot." We threw it back and forth a few times until Tommy hit the hood of a producer's Mercedes convertible—while the producer was watching. We then resumed packing, and I asked Tommy how he liked the show.

"It was good, Daddy," he said, "but you lost."

"It was hard, my boy, and I was really nervous," I said.

"I know," he said. "I get nervous, too."

Later, my pals Barron and Steve had a dinner party for me at Morton's. As usual, conversation came slowly—this is Hollywood, after all. I sat in the midst of these revelers wondering what was going on in the heads of the poker-faced men. I was tired. I was extremely tired. Really, really tired.

Then the heavens opened up, revealing a shining heavenly light: my wife walked in with Tommy dressed in his Webelos uniform. ("We'll be loyal Scouts," in case you forgot.) Tommy was holding in his hand my hairbrush. He walked over to me *and said, "Daddy, you brush my hair the way you do. That's what makes it look best."*

In the middle of the meal, as conversation lagged once again, I said to Tommy, about six places away, "Come over here and kiss me, my boy." Amazingly, without a moment's argument, he got up, walked over, threw his arms around me, and kissed me. Happy Birthday.

The next morning Tommy awakened with a bad nosebleed, as he occasionally does when the air is very dry. Bright red arterial blood was running rapidly out of his nostrils. His mother mistakenly told him to lie down, and that only made the problem worse. Only when he sat up and applied many tissues to his nose did the bleeding stop.

"I don't like this," I said. "I'm taking him to the doctor." Unshowered, unshaved, looking like an Iranian revolutionary on the morning after, I rushed him to his doctor in Beverly Hills. Tommy was still wearing the Webelos uniform he had slept in. The doctor, in typical modern fashion, pronounced Tommy fit without even looking in his nose or ears or throat. When I reminded her of this curious lapse, she examined the patient as directed and again said there was nothing wrong with him.

We left the doctor's office and went for breakfast—just us two Damon Runyon characters out on the town—at a tiny deli on Camden Drive. Then I took Tommy, who voluntarily held out his hand to be held by me, five or six blocks to his barber. On some blocks on that morning in Beverly Hills, there was no one on the street but Tommy and me. The sun was blindingly bright. The air was warm and dry. I felt as if I were walking down the gilded streets of heaven hand in hand with an angel. I could remember, but only just, how it felt, maybe seven years earlier, to see other dads confidently strolling with their kids and how much I wished I could do the same. Now I was in the circle. I felt like a twenty-game winner, like a Heisman Trophy winner.

Truth to tell, for most of my lengthy tenure in Los Angeles I felt a little intimidated and revolted by Beverly Hills. It seems to be populated by people who have some effortless gift for making huge amounts of money and spending it, and then making more. This is a gift I do not have. Beverly Hills is also filled with people who look much, much tougher than I will ever be, and toughness is a quality much in demand in Los Angeles.

On this day, though, I had the keys to the kingdom right in my hand. As my son and I passed an antique shop, the salesgirl came out to the sidewalk; she told us her brother was a Cub Scout, then added that he did not look as cute as Tommy did in his uniform. We thanked her and walked on.

"Tommy," I said, "you look like a god in that uniform. I hope you know that."

"Daddy," he said evenly, "that's in your *eyes."*

A modest god.

After his haircut, I took Tommy to school, gave instructions to his teacher about what to do if he had a nosebleed, and then went back to my solitary office to work. I felt like Cinderella after the ball—back in rags, with a pumpkin, not a chariot, nearby.

Two days after that was Thanksgiving. In the morning I took Tommy to play basketball at a park near our house. It was filled with Russian immigrants, madly playing chess and smoking cigarettes. We played basketball with some little Russian boys and two adults who lived nearby. Basketball is the only sport in which I retain some minimal competence. Tommy watched openmouthed as I made shot after (very easy) shot.

After a half hour, the other players left and Tommy and I were left playing horse against each other.

After we had played several games, I told Tommy it was time to go and get ready for our Thanksgiving dinner. "Daddy," he said, "why can't we just stay here all day and not have Thanksgiving dinner? I just want to stay here and play basketball with you." I know this shows my age and my particular weaknesses, but when my son said that, it sounded more melodious to me than when any woman ever said, "Yes and yes and yes."

On our way to Thanksgiving dinner, Alex and I sat in the front of the car. "I feel so tired," I said to her. "So unbelievably tired."

"That's how I feel," said Alex. "Just unbelievably tired."

In the back seat, Tommy sat up and asked, "Mommy and Daddy, are you aliens?"

The party was at the magnificently huge home of the family of Fred Savage, star of my favorite show The Wonder Years. *Fred was then a junior at Stanford. His younger brother Ben, age sixteen, was the star of* Boy Meets World. *His parents and his sister are incredibly kind people who do still have the gift of conversation. But I was staggered by the size of the house; it could have accommodated several of ours. The other guests were pleasant but, for some reason, a bit difficult to talk to. Tommy grew restless and began to spill his food. Then he noticed a basketball. Lew, Fred's father, saw Tommy's glance. "We have a basketball hoop set up," he said. "Tommy can play if he wants."*

It turned out that the Savages not only had a basketball hoop but also had a whole tennis court with a basketball hoop at one end. Warm Santa Ana winds were sweeping across Encino, rustling the palms near the court. The sodium vapor lights gave a pinkish daylight feel to the game even at nine at night in November. Tommy and I played for an hour while the grown-ups inside ate their turkey and talked about real estate.

When I had made several layups in a row, Tommy asked me, in a perfectly serious tone, "Daddy, can you dunk it from above the rim?" I felt light-headed. In the bath of sodium vapor brilliance, with the warm wind blowing down from the desert, my boy asked me if I, a fifty-two-year-old overweight man who stays in bed most of the day, could dunk the basketball from above the rim. "Like Michael Jordan," he continued.

Thanksgiving.

EIGHT

The nucleus of the atom of my life is my love and duty to Tommy. At first I was terrified of the relationship; I dreaded that I would fail at it and that it would pull me to pieces. Instead, that relationship has been and is so wholesome and so dense with sanity that it has reorganized all of the other relationships in my life.

Example: I see how totally important Tommy is to Mommy and me. This tells me that it makes a lot of sense to show extreme devotion to my own parents. In the past five or six years, I formed the habit of visiting my parents in Washington, D.C., at least once a month. It would have been up to them to say what that means to them, but it surely has meant a lot to me to know that I was acting right to them. I spoke to them on the phone every day, kept in touch with everything they did hour by hour. I made sure I read every one of the torrent of words my father writes and that I thought about them and commented back to him about them in detail.

This kind of behavior does not even seem like an effort, any more than spending as much time as possible with Tommy is an effort. I have come to think there might be something innate in the human soul that tells us when what we are doing is right and when it is wrong. When we do the right thing, we just feel good, not guilty and ragged. When I stayed up with my parents watching the tennis from Queens on TV until they fell asleep, I walked across Virginia Avenue from The Watergate back to my hotel with a spring in my step. When I called them and talked to them for an hour when they were housebound by bad weather, I felt as if I were doing something useful with my life. That's also the way I felt most of the time I spent listening to my parents talking about their college days in the Great Depression or watching the twentieth rerun of *Murder She Wrote* or playing Jeopardy! as we ate a Spartan dinner. Relationships with parents are crucial. That's true for Tommy and me, and true for my parents and me. I learned it from my life with my boy.

My mother, God bless her, entered immortality on April 21 of 1997. I learned about it on a flight from LAX to New York to have Passover with my family. I felt sick about my loss for some time, but I was fairly sure I had done my best by my mother. It would have been hard for anyone who did not have a private jet to have spent more time with her or been more attentive. That is, my behavior towards her in her later years is not in the catalog of sins I review at three in the morning. I credit what I have learned from my life with Tommy for understanding how to act towards my mother. I now spend even more time with my father, living alone at this point after losing his life mate of sixty years. This, too, I believe I came to understand from what I now see of what a family should be, that is, from lessons learned from being around my Tommy boy.

Likewise, I would not have Tommy if not for my wife. She did most of the legwork to find the blessed lawyer, David

Radis, who found Tommy's mother. When I was misbehaving in the months after we brought Tommy home from Kansas City, Alex took care of him. She never held it against me that I was not around. She worked little by little, with ultimate gentleness and consideration, to bring Tommy and me together. She never preaches to me about him and approaches his upbringing with extraordinary good humor. She is a genius at constructing the mother–father–son relation, never intruding too far between Tommy and me but also displaying exactly the right amount of presence of the Mommy function (at least as I see it).

Tommy has picked up exactly Alex's sense of finesse and gentility in his speech and observations. For example, when he sees someone driving horribly on the freeway (much of life here consists of being on the freeway and observing terrifying driving), he says, "Daddy, is that person an idiot?" He has picked up exactly Alex's superb sense of humor. Recently, when his new cat—a rescue made by my wife of a screaming kitty someone had run over near Paramount—pooped under his bed, he pointed out the evidence and said to his mom, "Would you care to do the honors?" When I told him it was an honor for him to be able to clean up after the cat and shoulder part of the family duties, he said, "It's an honor I am not worthy of." When Tommy asked on Thanksgiving if we were aliens, Alex went into a lengthy explanation of how all of us, Tommy included, were indeed aliens. Tommy picked up the joke and went along with it as if he were Jay Leno interviewing an alien. For these gifts to me and to Tommy, I must be humbly grateful to my wife, and I am.

At the most basic level, when I consider how meaningless my life would be without Tommy and how I wouldn't have him without Alex (or "the Saint," as I call her), I have to act a lot better to her than I did for most of our lives together. I cannot afford to build her a Taj Mahal, but I make my thanks as I can. I have given up almost all displays of anger, a former major cause of discord in our lives, even when I get a stunningly large bill for some bauble she has bought or when she accidentally throws away a vital residual that arrived that morning. You do not pick fights over a missing check or a MasterCard bill (unless it's over ten thousand dollars for one month) with someone who has saved your life. You value the woman who gave your life meaning unless you are really insane (which I sometimes still am).

I make it a point to praise Alex to Tommy on every possible occasion. I often tell him, truthfully, that his mommy is the smartest woman in the world. Whenever any opportunity arises, I explain to him how lucky he is to have such a mild-mannered, good-natured mother. Luckily for me, sometimes when Alex subtly points out my faults—often having to do with a basic inability to learn lessons—Tommy interrupts her. "Mommy," he says, "Daddy never says anything but good things about you."

The relation between the Saint and me is fundamentally different now that we have Tommy as the guiding star in our firmament. It's no longer about me first and the devil take the hindmost. We have a higher purpose now—the raising of Little Perfect—and that takes almost all of the competition and tension out of our lives, except as it relates to raising our son properly and, above all, safely. Our life together is calm.

The same goes for my relationships with my friends. I have always valued friends extremely highly. In many ways, they are modern life's equivalent of family, especially when you live far from most of your close relatives, as I do. But now that Tommy is here, I want to be extra good to my friends. For one thing, I want Tommy to see how good it is to have friends. I hope to show him by precept and example just how great it is to have people around that you can talk to and turn to in case of emergency or loneliness or just when you have a need for companionship. Everyone knows that there are times when you get more out of the reassurance of a friend than from family. Friends often know your life better, do not hold you to such a rigorous standard, and forgive faster than family. For another thing, friends are the framework on which a life outside the family begins to be built. You get your first start in life from your family, at least in ideal circumstances. But after family, friends are the future source of jobs and social relations and counsel. When I look back, I can see that every job I got when I was a young man came from a referral or connection from some family friend. My jobs at the *Washington Post,* at the prestigious law firm of Arnold & Porter, at the White House, at *The Wall Street Journal*—all of these and many more came from friends of me old ma and pa. I hope to bequeath to Tommy friends who might help him as well. Most important of all, I cannot in any sense count on living for any given span of years. When I shuffle off this mortal coil, I want Tommy to have friends who will help him from a feeling of gratitude and affection for me.

For Tommy's sake, I also have to feel rooted in society at large. I want to leave Tommy what Othello valued so highly: a good name. I want him to be identified with a name that speaks of hard work and honest behavior, so that friends and strangers will want to have good things to do with him. My father, a thousand times harder working and more rigorously honest than I have been, left that name to me and it has helped immensely. I want to pass it on as untarnished as possible to Tommy. That means I have to play fair and square and make my life into a reputable little cell in the body of the community—however tempted I may be to do otherwise. Again, that's so Tommy will have a place in the world that he can step into, a place that will shelter him and nurture him and keep him from being just a lonely soul hustling and scuffling out there on a smile and a shoe shine.

This means that if I have a deal with a studio, I do my part as well as I can and I don't stint on effort or complain (unless it's absolutely necessary). If I am working with a publisher, I do the best I can, never ask for unnecessary expenses, refrain from starting fights over little things (or even big things), and express as much interest in my editor's life as he does in mine. If an advertising executive remembers my birthday, I remember his. If she has kids, I ask about them when she asks about Tommy. If she sends me a poinsettia, I send her a wreath. If she needs help on a budget, I take it easy on my fee. If I'm acting, I don't throw a fit if I don't have a clean dressing room, I don't complain about working late, and I learn the assistant director's name.

Interestingly enough, this effort to act right is not a burden. Having decent relationships with my family, friends, and the community makes my life easier and more pleasant, not less so. Or, to put it differently, I find that once my relationship with my son is right (or at least when I am trying to make it right), my other relationships improve dramatically. If my relationship with Tommy is right (in terms of giving him enough attention and support and encouragement and discipline and just plain time), my relationship with my wife is right—or at least as right as it can be day by day. If my relationship with my son is right, my relationship with my father (and, until recently, my mother) is right. If I am playing fair by Tommy, I play fair by my sister and her family.

Most of all, I would say that if my relationship with Tommy is right, my relationship with the community at large is right, or at least better. Taking care of Tommy is an organizing principle that works extremely well in my life.

About a week before Christmas 1996, I came down with a killing salmonella food poisoning. That malady is in a class by itself for unpleasant consequences, prolonged visits to the salle de bains, *and a feeling that you would be lucky if you died right then and there. For one whole day, I lay in bed listening to Mozart and passing in and out of consciousness. I decided that just in case I die from another attack of salmonella, I should write down in summary form a few of the elements of Tommy's life and mine that occur to me day by day as he passes through the magical transit of age nine.*

Start with the basic idea of paying attention to what's happening in the here and now.

When Tommy was about three years old, or maybe four, he started to make some stabs at tying his own shoelaces. This has never been an easy task for small children, and it was not for Tommy, either. Usually, he would just stick out his dainty little foot, and I would tie the lace. He would then daintily stick out the other, often while eating something like watermelon, with lots of juice and seeds. Then, when he was about four and a half, he started to get the hang of shoelace tying. My notion was that once he started trying to tie his shoes, he should just keep trying until he got it right. I would sternly encourage him to try over and over until he did it properly, here in Stein Boot Camp. My wife, on the other hand, worked on a different principle: She enjoyed tying Tommy's shoes. She threw herself into it when he showed the slightest hesitation. "Why are you doing this?" I would ask. "Why don't you let him do it?"

"Because some day he won't need me to tie his shoes," she said. "Some day he'll be grown up and he won't need us to do anything for him at all." She was right, of course.

Looking at Tommy's childhood as extremely brief has been one of the most valuable tools of fatherhood. That is, realizing that before I can say "tuition," he's going to be grown up, out the door, embarrassed even to be seen with his parents (let alone be seen holding his Dad's hand), greatly sharpens my appreciation of the moment.

Two nights ago, Tommy and I went to a famous deli in West Hollywood (not where I got my food poisoning, I am sure). I ran into some men I had known since 1985, when they were high school seniors and I sat in on their class at Birmingham High School in Van Nuys to write about modern education. The men are now successful TV writers. They sat with us and we talked about Hollywood and network meetings. As we did, Tommy made successively louder burping noises, and I kept shushing him. Then I looked over at my dinner companions. When I first met them, they were children. Now they are TV shtarkers. *Yet their high school days seem like yesterday. That's how it will be with Mr. Perfect, I thought. Today he's sitting here making burp sounds to get attention. Tomorrow I'll be calling him somewhere and his secretary will tell me he can't come to the phone right now because it's "just Dad." That's if I'm lucky. If I'm unlucky, he won't want to talk to me at all because he will be attending to his glorious career—as I once did.*

I stopped schmoozing and eating my corned beef and said, "Tommy, don't do burp sounds, but talk to us about anything you like." He's a spectacularly good conversationalist, and we soon learned that Tommy's fourth grade teacher was the girl-

friend of one of the young men. Tommy talked volubly with us about subjects of interest to all of us for another hour.

When Tommy wants me to sit with him and tell him a Ren and Stimpy story at night so he can sleep, it would be easy to tell him I'm too tired to think of a story for him. (By the way, thinking up a story that goes on for a long time and amuses Tommy and keeps Ren and Stimpy in character is not at all easy. It's mentally exhausting.) In fact, I often do tell him it's too tiring. But, in any event, I sit with him in the dark. The time is barreling down the pike when Tommy will not even consider having me sit in his room with him until he falls asleep. Plus, in my whole life, how many people are going to want me to sit with them and tell them stories? How many are going to sincerely tell me that they are afraid of the dark and need me in the room with them? In my whole life, is anyone else ever again going to cling to my leg and demand, plead, beg that I sit with him until sleep comes? *In all likelihood, when I am in a room at some low-rent nursing home or getting wheeled in for bypass surgery, I will think about all of the nights that Tommy begged for me to stay with him and tell him a Ren and Stimpy story. I will beg and plead with God Almighty to send me a dream about those nights. I am going to pay attention to these glorious moments right now. They will not last. They are like being present at a great historic event or the passing of a comet. I want to be all there for them.*

If Tommy wants me to sit on the edge of the bed with him and watch him play Nintendo 64 Star Wars until my eyes fall out of my head, I will do it as long as I can stay awake. It won't be long before I won't even know what he's doing day by day. It certainly won't be long before he won't want me looking over his shoulder while he does it. I am going to take advantage of the moment and appreciate it.

Every time I pick Tommy up at school, I feel conscious that in eight years—eight lightning-fast years that pass as fast as a week passed when I was young—Tommy will be going off to school if we're lucky. I will be so lonely that I'll feel as if I'm on Devil's Island. I am going to cherish the pleasure of picking him up right here and now, whether he looks like a slob, drags his backpack on the floor, or demands that we go to McDonald's, or forgets his homework.

Yes, it's totally maddening when I make him a hamburger and he then just leaves it uneaten when he plays his Nintendo (brain crack for nine-year-olds). But the time will come when I won't even see him for days on end. Maybe for months on end. I am going to be grateful that he's here asking me for lunch, even if he doesn't eat it.

I believe that Tommy picks up my eagerness to spend time with him. It is genuine, so he should be able to feel it. If he does absorb it, he'll also internalize a strong base of how much I love him. Frankly, I do not think it's possible for him to feel too strongly that his father loves him and values him. There are those I respect who think that when a child senses such adoration, he gets spoiled and shiftless. I don't buy it. I believe that if Tommy knows that his mommy and daddy think he is the center of their lives—as he is—that will give him a sense of confidence, something every human needs. My need for my son's company, my appreciation of it—though "appreciation" is too mild a word—will give him the sense of worth and rootedness he needs. At least I hope so.

Another little item I hope to teach Tommy is to completely eschew contempt, to not even know what it is, and to have respect for himself as an individual. This will mark a difference with the way I was brought up.

When I was a child, I was a good student. But occasionally I had problems with my homework, especially with math. The concepts came easily, but I was too lazy to memorize the various ratios that came with plane geometry and solid geometry and, worst of all, trigonometry. Sometimes I asked my father for help. My father is an amazing genius, and in his later years, with Tommy and me, he is a patient teacher. You have to see him taking out his 1931 clarinet and showing Tommy how it works to see how patient he is. But when I was a child unable to figure out angles and sines and cosines, my father was not particularly patient. I guess he thought it was astonishing and wrong that a child of his should have trouble with math. It rapidly reached the point that I did not even bother to ask him for help.

I am determined to be more patient with Tommy than that. I do not want him to think that a question or even an error automatically elicits contempt. It is extremely natural to me to be contemptuous when people—including Tommy—fail to live up to my expectations. I have already shown far more contempt for Tommy's errors than I should have. I see the results in his occasional contemptuous judgments of others, especially those who are not similarly situated. This really upsets me a lot. It's definitely a reflection of my own failings as a human being and is the unfortunate passing on from one generation to the next of habits of contempt. It is a desperate wish of mine to turn that around, to teach Tommy patience with others and with himself. Unless he's a lawyer and has to worry about contempt of court, "contempt" should be like a word in a foreign language that he does not even know. Bob Butler, a very smart shrink in Washington, D.C., once told me that the single best lesson he could give me was to "forget contempt," an attitude that comes back on the person who employs it. That's a fate I would like for Tommy to avoid.

Likewise, the emotional fact that caused me the most misery when I was a child was the oppressive comparisons with others made by my mother. I am sure she did it to spur me to greater efforts in school—a good goal, since such efforts usually make life easier. But her endless refrain was that I should look to what Jerry Akman or Stanley Sitnick or Jeffrey Burt or another classmate was doing in school, should study as hard as those students did. When I brought home a report card, she studied it and then asked how Jerry Akman, Stanley Sitnick, and Jeff Burt had done. If they had done better, I was in for major anger. I cannot think about the boys whose names my mother endlessly brought up to me without wincing even now. My mother undoubtedly meant well, but the effect was and is painful.

My job with little Mr. Perfect is to make sure he studies and to do my best to get him on the road to a good education but to do it so that he knows he is valued for his own individual light. It's true that Tommy is—or used to be—occasionally lazy. But it's also a fact that he has an amazing gift with words and vocabulary. He's already correcting me on the difference between "wants" and "needs," already telling me when to use "which" and when to use "that." It's true that he cannot write numbers legibly unless I hold a sledgehammer to his head, but it's also true that he thoroughly reads the instructions to his Star Wars or Mortal Kombat III or Cruisin' USA video games before he punches a single button (in this respect he is far, far ahead of his father and mother, for whom instructions for appliances might as well not exist). Tommy is dismayingly resistant to reading about history—an obsession of the other men in the Stein family—but he will study a diagram of an electric motor for hours and understand its workings far better than I could.

Tommy is also an amazingly good con man and debater, although this may be a common characteristic of his age and the state of society. His ability to persuade me to buy him a motorboat, not just one but several mountain bikes, and, most recently, a Wave Runner is startling to me even as I feel the cash getting sucked out of my wallet.

He is his own boy. When I tell my son he has to do his homework, I never tell him he has to do it so he can do as well as his friend Christopher or his friend Alex or his friend Jake. He has to do it for his own future and his own self-respect. I would rather leave him with the idea that he is his own man and is prized for who he is than leave him ten million dollars. (Both would be good, though.) I never tell him he has to bend his every muscle to get into Harvard (a favorite refrain of my mother's). I want him to get into a good college, but I never want him to feel that he will be a failure if he doesn't. He may want to go to art or design school or maybe to West Point, like his maternal grandfather. He might want to take to the sea and sail around the oceans. I want Tommy Stein to succeed as the best possible Tommy Stein, *not as some other little boy. If he can value himself as an individual and also never be a charge on society, I will be really happy.*

I would also love to teach my son that life is hard and some mistakes are inevitable. If I ever give him the impression that anyone we know is even remotely close to perfection, then shame on me. For Tommy Stein, I hope the only distinctly negative association will be with lack of effort and unethical behavior. Failure, even frequent failure, will be a constant in his life as it is in all lives. I would like for him to see failure as just a part—but only a part—of the wallpaper of human exis-

tence. I want him to see unethical behavior as a disgrace and a sign of weakness.

I also want to make sure Tommy knows that unhappiness will also be a large part of his life. He does not always have to be bubbly and "up." He does not need to have a "take-charge" and "can-do" attitude. He can feel sad or grumpy or out of sorts on occasion, even on frequent occasion. That's life for everyone, not just for him. He should not be surprised if he spends many hours feeling sad. That is just how life is, and if he learns to expect it, he'll be less bothered by it. Above all, if he has the idea that unhappiness is a condition that comes and goes like a cold or an allergic reaction, he will be less tempted to drug himself to avoid the feeling. Men and women who know that after a nap or a good night's sleep most feelings of sadness and desperation disappear are far less likely to wind up needing a pill or a drink for every problem that crosses the radar screen.

Another piece of data I would like for Tommy to know is Daddy.

Example: A few days ago, when I was picking Tommy up at school, I told him I had to rush over to do a voice for a cartoon he loves called Rugrats. *He sulked and did not want to go. "It's boring," he said. "I want to play with my video games."*

I got extremely angry at him for that. I told him I would throw away all of his video games to punish him for insulting me. Then I told him I wondered if he knew just how insulting he was being to the whole father–son relationship. "I'm Daddy," I said. "I take care of you. I feed you. I tuck you in. I help you with your homework. I take you to soccer. When you're upset, I cheer you up. I take you to Idaho for the summer. Along with Mommy, I am the one who makes sure you're all right. My whole life's work is to make you safe."

Tommy looked sullenly ahead in the car. At moments like this, all of my good resolves vanish and I am left with my own lack of perfection and his. I really want to hit him.

"Not only that," I said, barely restraining myself from smacking him, "but I have lived a fairly interesting life. I've met Elvis. I've worked for two presidents. I was in the thick of the sixties. I have been in a lot of movies. To college students, I'm a cult figure because of Ferris Bueller. *I think I might be worth your paying attention to. Plus, I am attuned to your every mood, and that might make me a better conversationalist than most of the people you deal with. I have a lot to tell you about me, about you, about life. I think that makes me more interesting than a goddamned video game."*

Tommy did not look thoroughly convinced, but that's all right, too. My talk had put me in mind of something basic. I want to make sure that Tommy knows who I am, who his mother is, who his grandparents are, where he came from.

Too many kids—even middle-aged kids—lose their parents and then lament that they never knew who their parents were. "I wish I had known him better," they say about their fathers. "I wish he had told me about his life and what was in his heart."

I want to obviate that problem with Tommy Stein. If it's possible, I would like for him to know that his maternal grandfather was a major-league war hero who fought hand to hand against the SS in southern Germany. Tommy should know that this same man in middle age was in desperate firefights against the North Vietnamese in swampy rice paddies. He should know that his grandfather on my side rose from total obscurity to become one of the nation's most distinguished economists and social thinkers. He should know of his grandmother's bravery in following her Army husband from town to dusty town to help him make his Army career. He should have some idea that his paternal grandmother was a brilliant student of economics who made a name for herself in late middle age as a defender of a very misunderstood president.

I would also pray that he understands some day the exaltation his Mommy and I felt when we graduated from law school. It's good for him to know that his parents—not just his grandparents—did something fairly difficult and had a good lift of pride when it got done. Some day he might derive some encouragement from thinking that if his lumbering old folks could do it, maybe he can do it, too. The example of a parent is immediate, at least for me and my wife, and maybe it will be for Tommy, too.

I want my son to know my feeling of fear and confusion when we were demonstrating against segregated restaurants in Maryland long ago. I would like for him to know every word of "We Shall Overcome" and know what it meant to sing it. He should have some idea that although I, like every other middle-aged man, have got to be consumed largely by the chase for the almighty dollar, I have also had some measure of idealism in my life. How I want Tommy to understand the days when we sang civil rights songs in front of the Lincoln Memorial so that each individual could be treated as an individual and not damned because of his or her status at birth. It would be grand if he had in his mind that crystal of an idea: that the greatness of our century has been the move from regarding each man or woman as part of a certain stratum of society to regarding each as having infinite potential as an individual in a free society.

I would like for Tommy to see me staying up late at night to do my cursed taxes or to meet a deadline for even a small article so that I could get paid and then pay my bills. I want him to see that if a restaurant makes a mistake on a bill in my favor, I pay it back to them. Maybe it's possible for a child to learn virtue from reading a book about it; maybe it's possible, and I sure wish I had thought up the idea for it. But I feel certain that Tommy can learn some measure of virtue if he sees his father behaving virtuously. True, I am the world's biggest starer at women. True, I often make slighting remarks about bad drivers. True, I even fall into the evil trap of racism on occasion. But I hope that Tommy never sees me chisel, never sees me steal. If he knows that it's just the Stein and Denman family way not to take what does not belong to us, I think he has learned something about who he is. Years ago, when someone on a construction site left out a board and my mother fell on it and hurt her knee, I asked her if she was going to sue. "Of course not," she said.

"Why?" I asked.

"Because we're not that kind of people," she said.

My father has never in his entire life sought out a penny except for work honestly done. Neither has my wife or my father-in-law. I would like for Tommy to know that this is what he came from and who he is.

I am the world's worst golfer, bar none. But I do know how to hold the club properly. I do know how to address the ball. And when I hit it in the rough, I "play it as it lays," to coin a phrase. When Tommy plays, it's an endless fight to get him to hold the club properly, line up his feet correctly, and concentrate on the ball. It's also hard to make him keep score. But if I can just get him to learn that the Steins may not be the best players (or even average players) but that we play by the rules, I will consider him a good golfer. I don't want him to be a skillful gamester. I want him to follow the rules of the game and to know that's how his dad and his ancestors did it.

I have taken Tommy to the redwood forests behind the glorious University of California at Santa Cruz and plan to take him there again and again so he can smell that fragrance of dried redwood, see the glittering Monterey Bay, watch the deer wander through the ferns and shadows, and know what it meant to me to experience these things all those years ago when I escaped from law practice in a dingy windowless cubicle. In words my father and I often share, I want my son to learn that there is beauty on this earth and that his eyes should be open to that beauty as much as they can be. We can and do get into that basic concept of the uplifting quality of the beautiful when we are on the lake in Idaho, but there is no such thing as too much beauty. Boys sometimes think there is something wrong with them if they appreciate the beauty in nature. I do not want Tommy to be so burdened. I want him to know and love and be buoyed up by the glory that God has put around us.

I especially want Tommy to know that Daddy is often depressed, lonely, sad, alarmingly weak, pathetically self-doubting, and often in a deep funk for weeks on end. He should know that there are situations that have stymied his large father. I would like for him to know that, so that when he is older and he is balked, he will know that he is not alone and that his condition is a basic of the human situation—at least in the little Stein family. He must know that he is not irresponsible if he exults and that he is not weak—or at least not uniquely weak—if he is blocked and sad. He must know that life is not always easy and that we often feel humbled by it and, worse, defeated by what we have done to ourselves.

I don't expect Tommy to write my biography. I do hope that he will be cushioned by the knowledge that his father, mother, and all of his other ancestors have been there before him—to some of the bad places as well as the good ones. Someday down the pike, when he has lost a job or a girlfriend or a bout with his self-respect (or is struggling with his taxes), I would like for him to know that his ancestors walked down the same muddy streets and sat in the same dim rooms wondering if we had any future at all. And yet we did. And Tommy is the most golden, shining avatar of that future.

If Tommy knows where he came from and that he came from a good place, but a place shared by humanity in our weakness and failure, he will be far better off than most kids. That is something I definitely want for him. (And then I would like for the other kids to catch up.)

NINE

Three days before New Year's Eve, 1996, Tommy went off to Philadelphia with his mom to see her sister and her family. I took them to the airport and then stayed with them until they boarded their plane. At the airport Tommy bought some new Beanie Babies, a fad for little kids. These are small stuffed toys that represent various animals. Tommy has dozens of them but needed more to keep him company on the plane. He showed me his shopping bag of Beanie Babies and took out a little pink pig doll. "I'm going to call you the same name as this Beanie Baby," Tommy said with a big smile. "His name is Oink." (I told you he was a character.) I was so sad at his departure that I was already missing him and didn't even reproach him for that joke (I hope it was a joke). Instead, I watched him and Mommy get on the airplane, waved goodbye, and then felt so lonely that I just sat by the gate for a half hour until the plane had left the gate and disappeared to some remote part of the runway system of mighty LAX.

When I got to my car, I called in for my messages. Both of my machines were full of messages—all of them from two different women. (I am surrounded by women looking for Daddy.) One of the women, a startlingly beautiful Audrey Hepburn look-alike, is in her early thirties. She lost her father to divorce when she was five and never saw him again. She is still traumatized, still lost, still mourning, still hurting herself in many cruel ways. She met me some years ago and has adopted me as a father figure. Now she calls me constantly during holidays and on beautiful days in the spring to tell me how lonely she is. "I still miss my father," she said in about a hundred different ways on her messages. "You come over and tell me stories."

The other set of messages was from a woman named Shoshonna, the daughter of Holocaust survivors. She, at forty-two, became a single mother after an affair with a married man. The man had not wanted children and is very far from being an enthusiastic father. After prolonged litigation, Shoshonna got a modicum of child support and a promise from the father to spend one afternoon every other Sunday with the little boy, Martin Luther. The little boy is amazingly sweet and smart. He picks up every mood and nuance around him. Martin (according to his mother) repeatedly asks why he cannot have his mother and father together the way other boys' parents are. He keeps asking men he sees in stores if they are his daddy. He often asks me if I am his daddy. "You can think of me as Ben, your special pal," I have often said to him, "but I am really not your father."

Shoshonna left me a number of messages asking me if I could see her and Martin Luther on this inter-holiday Saturday and buy him a TV. (Shoshonna, whatever her other qualities, is not at all shy about asking for things.) I met mother and son at an appliance store late in the afternoon. The little boy was eagerly staring at the TVs. I picked an inexpensive one, bought it for him, and then asked him if he wanted to have dinner. "I want to go home with you, Ben," he said sweetly.

I took mother and son back to my house and made them spaghetti in the microwave and steaks on the gas grill. Martin Luther, God bless him, stayed out on the deck with me and the steaks, "helping" me and keeping me company while Shoshonna ate the spaghetti I had supposedly made for him. When I laid the steaks, potatoes, and string beans on the table, my two dogs, Ginger and Susan, stood and watched while Martin ate his Omaha beef processors' meat, sent to me by two pals through the miracle of mail order. After Martin Luther had his fill of steak, he opened his arms wide and said, looking first at me and then at his Mommy, "Now we have everything we need, because this is my whole family."

A few minutes later, in the kitchen as I cleaned up, he said again, while hugging Ginger, "This is my whole family." He went from one of us to the other, hugging each of us in turn. When he started to fall asleep, he wanted to lie down on a love seat in the living room, within close proximity to the dining room so that he could see us. Repeatedly, he sat up and said, "I'm still awake. I'm still here with my family."

When the time came for them to leave, Shoshonna roused her son. As he stumbled out the door, he asked, "Aren't you coming, Ben-Daddy?" "I'm afraid not," I said. "I have to take care of the dogs and the cat tonight."

Martin started to cry and sat down on the step in front of the door.

The next morning, Shoshonna called me to tell me that the little boy—age two, mind you—had slept in his own bed for the first time ever that night, had gotten up to turn on "my TV that Ben-Daddy gave me," and had watched cartoons on it until she awoke. Thank you, God, for letting me be there for that child.

That morning also, Little Perfect called me from Philadelphia to tell me about life with his cousins. "He's just impossible," Alex told me. "No matter what his cousins say, he says, 'Well, my Daddy says such and such.' And no matter what I try to tell him to make him go to sleep, he says, 'No, tell me a story just like the ones that Daddy tells me. It has to be like Daddy's.' And whenever one of the other kids says anything, he says, 'Well, when my Daddy and I were in Idaho this summer, we did more sailing or rode better mountain bikes or drove on more dangerous roads.' It's like he's addicted to Daddy." After Alex told me that, I got up, went into Tommy's little room, lay on his twin bed, and felt that I had arrived. On the floor was a year's worth of toys (Tommy had pulled them all out of his closet in order to select what he wanted to take on his trip.) All around on the floor were his discards of clothes, and under the bed was Peabo, his cat. I breathed Tommy air until I fell asleep. Happy New Year.

On a day in January of 1997, my wife awakened with a sore throat, as she often does. She stayed in bed. Tommy resisted getting up mightily and said the magic words, "I want to spend the day with you, Daddy. What are we doing today?"

My first thought was that I would be a total failure and gangster if I did not take him to school. Then I thought that I had an interesting day planned. If Tommy were a girl, and if I were a woman who worked, I would be praised, rather than blamed, if I took him to my work with me. So I decided to begin the custom of Bring Your Son to Work Day in the Stein family.

When I was a child, I rarely saw what my father was doing at his work. One result was that I was terrified of the whole concept of adult work, since I had no idea of what it was. (It seemed to mostly consist of sitting in an office and looking out the window, inhaling a Kent cigarette, and then writing on a lined pad.) I want Tommy to have a slightly more exact idea of what adult work might be.

So I got Tommy dressed, fed, and out the door (and was exhausted already from that struggle). Our first stop was a tiny voice-over studio in Studio City. There, with Tommy showing almost zero interest, I auditioned for the part of a bathroom drain in a commercial for Liquid-Plumr. My job was to sound stuffed up and unhappy until I got my shot of Liquid-Plumr. Frankly, it was not an easy spot to do, since I well know that Liquid-Plumr—a fine product I often use—is strong acid. The thought that I might feel better if I drank a quart of acid was not easy to get into my mind.

Tommy's only comment was that he wanted to play Ping-Pong.

Then we headed to the freeway on a perfect, glorious day and aimed for our ramshackle home in Malibu. Rain had fallen in Los Angeles for about two solid weeks until the day before. The hills along Malibu Creek were literally glowing with green grass. "Look, Tommy! The hills are so incredibly green."

He looked and said, "How does that happen, Daddy?"

"I think it has to do with nutrients in the rainwater and also with the water dissolving nitrogen and other minerals in the soil, and they get into the plants and make the plants green." This was a dim memory from Botany 101 at Columbia in 1963.

Tommy gazed at the riot of green for a long time. Soon the ocean came into view. It was a stunning deep blue. Tommy looked at it for a long time, too, and then said, "Daddy, when we get to our house, can you help me attach some video games to the TV?"

"No, my boy," I said. "It is far too beautiful for you to play indoors." Then I said, "But I will give you a lecture about Adam Smith's immortal book, The Wealth of Nations.*" Then I told him that Adam Smith explained how the free market works and why it's so superior to the command economy. "In a way, it's because in our free society men and women are told they can do what they want. They do not have to be coal miners or steelworkers or doctors or teachers. They do what they want, and the forces of the market guide them."*

"Does that mean I get to do anything I want?"

"It does when you're out of school," I said, "and when you are self-supporting."

"Can I be a race car driver then?"

"No, because Adam Smith said that smart people never do anything that could hurt them for no good reason. And he said it was up to their parents to guide them in this regard until they reached the age of at least forty."

Tommy took this in unquestioningly. Then I told him about Smith and free competition and allowing the market to ration goods and services so that, for example, the more popular Nintendo 64 games would command a premium in price over the less popular SEGA games and thus the market would command the production of more Nintendo games and fewer SEGA games until there was an improved SEGA system.

"I wish SEGA and Nintendo would merge and make one big company that would make the best video games in the world," Tommy said.

"Well, you're not quite getting it," I said. "Smith wanted competition. He thought that if there were just one big video game company, it would make an inferior product and would

fix prices at an artificially high level. That was what a lot of his writing was about."

I explained this for a long time. I am not at all certain that Tommy "got" it. I am sure that when he is in Econ 101 and The Wealth of Nations *comes up, he will have some familiarity with it and will have some confidence that he can understand it, because his daddy explained it to him long ago on a highway next to a deep blue ocean.*

At home I rested on my deck overlooking the mighty Pacific while Tommy, despite the utmost moral suasion, played video games in his room. After a couple of hours, Tommy and I went off to Pepperdine, where I teach law. The weather had turned cool and, of course, Tommy had forgotten a sweatshirt. I bought him a Pepperdine Law School sweatshirt, and he sat in class occasionally making faces at me and occasionally playing his video game. At the class break, he played Ping-Pong with a boy in the class and beat him (Tommy has a demonic serve).

After class, Tommy and I drove over to Sony Studios in Culver City in astounding traffic. We wandered around the darkened former MGM lot for a half hour and finally found the spot where I was to do a voice-over for a movie. Tommy, of course, ran around the control room seeing what he could break. Several longtime friends appeared on the scene and supervised my reading. Then Tommy and I walked back down the fake Main Street of Sony Studios and headed east.

Through still heavy traffic, we ventured out onto the Santa Monica Freeway and towards downtown. We drove to the Los Angeles Athletic Club, an old downtown club of which I am a member. (I love that club because it is the only private downtown club that has always admitted members regardless of race, ethnicity, religion, or sex. More of that wonderful move from status to contract.)

At the club we showered and got into our bathing suits. Tommy had to race back and forth from the steam room to the cold plunge. "This makes my nuts like ice!" he gasped to me each of the four times he went into the cold plunge. Then to the immense old pool for Tommy to finish a scouting requirement. For his Webelos Swimmers' Badge Tommy had to pass several tests: He had to do a surface dive, then swim for thirty seconds underwater, and then swim using two different strokes. He had to swim four Olympic lengths. At the Los Angeles Athletic Club that day Tommy had to demonstrate to me three ways of saving a swimmer in distress: carry, reach, or toss a flotation device. He did them all flawlessly and then swam leisurely back and forth. Another merit badge for Webelos Tommy Stein. And another time the club has come in handy. I was mindful of the months my wife and I had spent taking him to swimming lessons and how what seems so effortless for Tommy in the pool really took so much time and investment by Mom and Dad—and even some by Tommy. The dividend, of course, is that effortless little god in the pool.

After swimming, Tommy and I had dinner in a deli at the club while we played chess. Tommy has become a decent player (by my modest standards). Again, I was struck by how good he is and how many, many hours it took for me to teach him how to play (so that soon he will be able to beat me).

Then, back home. Mommy was still out cold, so Tommy and I used the word processor; I helped him write a story about exotic and sports cars and how much they cost. Then, to bed. "Daddy," he said, "tell me about something really boring to put me to sleep. Tell me about The Wealthy Nations *or whatever that famous book was."*

EPILOGUE

When I began writing this book in the summer of 1996, I was at our rented house on Lake Pend Oreille in Sandpoint, Idaho. My routine was that I would get up before my son and go down to the dining room to write until he awakened. Then I would make him breakfast, after which we would get dressed and go about the day.

Our rounds usually involved bicycling across the Long Bridge over the Pend Oreille River, stopping on the other side at Swan's Landing for lunch, and heading back and swimming in the lake for a while. Then we might rest or shop until late afternoon, when we would rendezvous with Peter Feierabend and his son, Alex, and use our boat. Peter would neatly take off the boat cover, fold it in a professional way, stow it on the dock, and cast off the lines. He would follow my every move at the helm, making sure we did not crash into another boat and keeping an eagle eye to ensure that we crossed the wakes of other boats at the proper angle, that we did not approach other boats too closely, and that we behaved like proper boatmen. When we got to a certain spot near Contest Point, a couple of miles across the lake from the marina, we would stop in front of a house that was built into a rock. Then Peter and the boys, and sometimes I, would jump into the chilly waters of the lake and swim around.

Many times, we brought a large tube with us. Tommy, Alex, or Peter would get into the tube, and I would pull it behind the boat, crossing our own wake to make the tube and its rider fly into the air. Then we would dry off and head to the cafe and marina at Bottle Bay and have dinner (meaning that Peter and I would have dinner while Tommy and Alex skipped rocks across the marina).

The sun set off to the west at the mouth of the bay. It was almost always sunset or just past sunset when we headed back to the marina in Sandpoint. Little insects were packed in dense formation on the surface of the water, and kokanee salmon leapt up in the spotlight of the boat to get them. Tommy and Alex jumped up and down or else hid in the cabin and told the dirty jokes little boys tell. "Drive slower," Peter would always say to me. "You have to be able to get out of the way of a log or a small boat that doesn't have any lights. Good decisions on the water. They're what keeps you alive."

On other nights we drove in my rented Caddy along the Pend Oreille River or by the Dufort Bypass to the Priest River and then up Route 57 to a far more remote spot, Priest Lake, and had dinner at Hill's Resort. Peter and I would sit gnawing on spareribs while Alex and Tommy played horseshoes on a grassy strip between the restaurant and the lake.

One night as we started to head up there from Sandpoint, Peter and I quarreled about what would be the faster route, Dufort Bypass or Pend Oreille River. We decided to race. When he beat me by less than he had predicted, he paid the wager by washing my windshield by hand. It was the cleanest my windshield had ever been. "There," he said, surveying his handiwork, "that works, doesn't it?"

Towards the end of that halcyon summer, Peter began to make preparations for a rafting adventure down the wild Salmon River. It was an elaborate adventure and it scared me to death. No phones, no doctors, no bathrooms. Peter laughed at my concerns. He was extremely eager to go and was not at all afraid of the lack of amenities. "That's a reason to go," he said, "not a reason to stay here."

The day before he left, I told him I was scared about the trip. Plus I was worried about his kids while he was gone. "Look," he said, "I've got to go. The kids are going to have to look after themselves."

That was an eerie announcement for someone whose plan was supposedly to be gone for only one week.

By the time Tommy and I packed our belongings and were ready to go for the end of summer, we still had not heard from Peter. Alex came to say good-bye and ran after the car to wave good-bye to Tommy. And then we were gone.

On September 13, 1996, I felt distinctly worried about Peter. I called and left a message for him. A few moments later, we got a call from Burdette Feierabend, Peter's former wife. Peter was missing and presumed drowned in the Salmon River or some damned river near Riggins, Idaho. Two days later the sheriff found his body.

Alex, Tommy, and I had already flown up to Sandpoint. We were with Peter's children, Rachel and Alex, when they learned the horrifying news. I held them both and felt their tears through my shirt. Three days after that, we had his body prepared for a viewing (Peter had not drowned but apparently had a heart attack after falling into the water).

After the body was cremated, I approached the children and told them that they were welcome to move to Los Angeles and live with us and that if they chose to stay in Sandpoint, we would make sure they were tided over materially until a modest inheritance came to them. They chose to stay in Sandpoint. I am in touch with them day by day except when they are traveling. Alex, the younger child, is desolate at night, his mother says, although he tries to be brave through the day. Rachel is also in a sort of long-lasting pain. I imagine, based on what I have seen, that this kind of trauma truly never stops. The kids are incredibly brave, but their loss is overwhelming.

As I watched the children staring at photos of their father at a memorial one month after the cremation, I was reminded of a line my old boss, Richard M. Nixon, said on the day he resigned. "Now, we look to the future. It's always a new beginning, always, whatever happens. The young must know it. The old must know it."

It's a new beginning for the children of one of the best teachers of fatherhood I could ever have had. In that new beginning, I get to pick up the baton he passed to me so many times. I get to teach the children of the teacher what the teacher taught me. It's unlikely that I can do it as well as Peter did. I lack his assuredness, the self-confidence that comes from being an all-American swimmer of the breaststroke. Still, I will try to be there for them. Not for "quality time," but for as much time as they need and as many flights down here on Alaska Airlines as they need. If I can be in any part as helpful to them as Peter was to Tommy and me, it will be a privilege.

The loss of Peter, out of nowhere, on a wild river in a wilderness, makes me realize that the journey of Tommy and me will also not go on forever. I am not a young man any longer. I drive the freeways every day. Anything can happen.

Tommy and I started this story in midair, and we are still in midair. I hope I have provided for his education and his comfort as he grows into manhood. But that's money. I really want to leave him what money cannot buy: an impression of what a human being should be to have some measure of self-respect in this world. My travels with Tommy are about laughter and amazement and anecdote. He never fails to astonish me (just two days ago he threatened to call 911 for child abuse if I pinched him for making fun of my voice).

But I would like for my son to have in him, along with his liver and his kidneys and his blood and his heart, some idea of how much he was loved, valued, even adored; of how precious he was to me, and is to everyone who gets to know him; of how well equipped God made him in brains and spirit and flesh to deal with whatever might happen to him.

Tommy, along with many others, especially Peter, has taught me to be a dad. It's by far the best job I have ever had and the most rewarding. I now know that my life would have been hollow without having been Tommy's dad.

Tommy, like Alex Feierabend and Rachel Feierabend, like all children, has a light surrounding him and coming out of him. I hope my parents got some illumination from my light, as I did from theirs. I have basked in Tommy's light for the last many years, and it has made my life far brighter than I ever dreamed it could be. I feel completely right only when I am with him, and feeling completely right is pretty good.

I hope I can travel with him forever in spirit. In a way, I feel only when I am with him that we can both stay, in the words of the poet, forever young. God bless that little angel and all who helped to bring us together.

APPENDIX
The Ten Commandments of Fatherhood

In the last five years, my main object has been to make sure I do the best possible job raising up Mister Perfect, Tommy Stein, my angel son, presently age ten. That means I have to be the best possible father I can be. I can only learn this from what turns out to be largely a trial-and-error course with Tommy, seeing what works to make him happy, confident, responsible, well-behaved, calm, and responsive.

I also observe what works with other fathers similarly situated. If they have kids who are getting along well in school, seem to be calm and without a frightened or dissimulated affect, if they play well and easily with other boys and girls and react well with their families, I seek to learn how they, the Dads, behave to get these results—or their part in these results.

Here is a brief summary of what I have seen that works in the Dad department. It applies to sons and daughters equally.

1. Time is of the essence. The number one keystone of being a happy child is spending a large amount—several hours per

day—with his Dad. You can't substitute for this by having just a few hours per week of "quality" time. It is far better, in terms of the strength of the child, to spend a lot of hours just sitting near him while he reads *Goosebumps* than a couple of hours every Saturday buying him expensive toys or taking in a movie.

This makes basic sense. When we are in love, we want to spend a lot of time with our love object, not just "quality" time. Whoever heard of a love affair where the lovers met only on Saturday afternoons for a couple of hours and called it "quality" time? This happens only in furtive, doomed affairs. Whoever heard of wanting only a little "quality" recognition for his work or achievement, or of wanting to spend only a little "quality" time doing the artistic work that is his pride?

A father's relationship with his child is one of his two most important relationships. It merits full-time attention and when it does, the Dad and the child get full-time results.

2. Share your strength with your child. Dads who raise successful kids do not raise them in fear. They use their Daddy-power to strengthen the child by sharing the Dad's power with the child. The Dad who is endlessly mindful that small children may act tough but are really afraid of the dark, afraid of being left alone, afraid of strangers—and need Dad's being with them to feel strong—gets a strong child.

This means that you are your child's ally, not his adversary. You share with him stories of your own fears, failings, anxieties. If your child is having a hard time with math, you do not mock and say you were a genius in math. You talk about areas where you had problems but got better and eventually mastered the subject.

The most encouragement I ever felt academically from my genius father was when he told me he had failed some test in graduate school—and then studied very hard and passed the next time with flying colors.

The child who knows his father was once afraid of the dark, too—and is still afraid of the doctor's needles—gets to know that his weaknesses are part of the common portion of mankind, not a unique source of shame. The child who sees that his big father also passes weak moments and hours knows that he can get through his dark times as well.

Daddy, to a child, is a tower of achievement and solidity. To let your child know that this tower of strength was once called "elephant ears" in third grade gives him confidence that no one else can give.

A child with a Dad as his ally is a strong child.

3. Do not expect your child to make up for your losses when you were a child. If you were a poor athlete in school, do not force your child to practice baseball or soccer for hours to redress your childhood feelings of inadequacy. If you were not well off as a child, do not feel that your child must show up in only the most expensive clothes and have every single fashionable toy. If you always wanted to be a star, do not make your child take acting lessons.

Your child has his own hopes and aspirations. To make him try to live up to yours is to deprive him of his own inner truth.

4. Look for the good in your child and praise it. Nothing is more readily done with a child than finding fault. Children are by nature messy, irresponsible, distracted, and uncommunicative. To discover these flaws or others like them would be, well, child's play. Obviously, when a child makes his room a total mess of candy and gum wrappers, unfinished games, and

dirty clothes, he has to be reminded to clean up. But when he does it right, he has to be praised. He has to be encouraged and rewarded for doing the right thing. Children generally do what they are encouraged to do. If you encourage your child to be neat, you will likely find that he is. If you mock him endlessly for being a mess, you might get a child who mocks in return but who is not necessarily tidy.

If your child is not great at English but is extremely sharp at science, you can build a platform for growth by noting his achievements in science. With the confidence that he can do well in one area, he can grow into others.

Encouragement is the primary engine of human development, at least for most children I see. Children need it at all ages of their lives. Even now, at 53, I derive great joy from my father's saying I know something valuable about any subject. When I was a child and my mother marveled at my singing ability, I was moved to sing constantly. Although no one else for many years has said I am a good singer, I still get great pleasure and peace from singing.

Children are nurtured by praise as plants are nurtured by water. Deny it to them at their peril and yours. Children who are told that they can succeed in fact usually do succeed.

5. Do not allow your children to be rude. I always tell my son that he can feel any way he wants. He can be sad or happy, energetic or slothful. This largely cannot be controlled. But how he acts toward those around him can be controlled. He is not allowed to turn his back on adults as he is talking to them, to fail to answer others when they greet him, to talk only about himself, to use other boys' toys and not share his own.

He is expected to show some respect for the pain of those around him, to congratulate those who succeed, to have some empathy for others' feelings. He is expected to know that while he is the apple of his Dad's eye, he is not the center of everyone else's universe.

By insisting upon something above minimum politeness, I make sure he gets some notion that others' feelings are worth taking into account. If he can get that into his little tow head, he will have learned the most basic foundation of human interaction. If I allowed him to grow up impolite and rude, I would condemn him to failure in almost every aspect of his life. I don't intend to let him go through life being despised for his surliness. I do not intend him to have a behavior flaw that ruins his life if I can help it, and I think I can.

6. Patience is indispensable. Children are not computers. Behavioral flaws cannot be corrected by flipping a switch or rewriting a few lines of code. You have to correct them a lot to get even the beginnings of improvement. This is standard. If you try to correct by force or terror, you get a terrorized child, not a correct child. Patience has the highest payoff of any virtue in dealing with children. This is not just because it takes account of what the child is by nature, but because if you are a patient Dad, you will get a patient child. If you are an impatient, demanding, short-fused Dad, you get that irritable, demanding kind of kid. The choice is largely up to you. I can tell you from my own experience, you definitely will want a patient child. You won't get one unless you are a patient Dad.

7. Teach your child and let him teach you. One of the most common errors about child development is that "kids don't come with instruction manuals." This simply is not true. Children do seem to come with an inner instruction manual. They tell you when they are hungry. They tell you

when they're lonely or scared or want company or want to play or want to be left alone. They are like little guided tours of themselves. Dads get into trouble when they do not listen to the child, when they think that if the child says he's scared, all the Dad has to do is say, "Don't be scared." Dads who think they can reply to a child's genuine needs by telling the child that they are not real or important or can simply be ignored get a highly confused—and sometimes extremely emotionally sick—child. Children will tell you what they want. Sometimes it's excessive. (No child needs every single video game ever made, but almost all will act as if they do.) But usually, a child can be counted on to tell you what he needs.

You deprive the child badly though if you do not tell him what you know and have seen of the world. Your child should get the benefit of your wisdom about life. You have to tell him that cars are dangerous and that drivers are far more dangerous, that money is highly explosive if you use it wrongly, that other human beings deserve respect, that rewards come from work, that honesty is the best policy for everyone in any transaction. You have to teach him that you love him, but will correct him when he does things that are bad for himself and others.

You hurt your child when you fail to heed what he knows about his legitimate needs. But you also hurt him when you do not teach him to respect his teachers, to drive with extreme defensive care in every situation, that being late to an appointment is nothing compared with being in a traffic accident.

Learn from your children and let them learn from you.

8. Value your child for what he is, not for what you think he should be. I find that when Tommy knows he is loved for himself and not for any particular accomplishment, he has a

certain peace that allows him to learn better, sleep better, play better, and be more helpful around the house. I want him to know that whatever he becomes in the future, he is prized just for being my son, right now. It is amazing but true that when I talk to him about that before he goes to sleep, he actually falls asleep faster than when we talk about something else.

Whether he becomes a rocket scientist or a plumber, a teacher or a sport fisherman, I want him to know he's number one with me. When Bill Cosby's son was murdered, Cosby said the exact right thing about his boy: "He was my hero." I want Tommy to know every day that he is his Dad's hero.

9. Raising a child is a job for Mom *and* Dad. It is hard work just to raise one child. To raise two or more is back-breaking physically, emotionally, and financially—even though it is uniquely rewarding. If you try to do it on your own, you are sunk beneath a tidal wave of work and worry. Now, as it happens, few Dads do have to do it alone, but many Moms do. This is deeply, horribly wrong. Dad should and must be in there pitching along with Mommy. Dad should stay there with Mommy, helping her out. The children are his as much as Mom's. Ethically, it is completely wrong to leave them with Mom in a divorce, separation, or unmarried situation. It is just plain criminal to blithely impregnate your lover and then walk away from the product, loving, perfect, but ultra-demanding.

Not only does leaving your kids alone with Mom for their youth painfully burden her, it hurts the kids indelibly. Children with absent fathers are wounded for the balance of their lives, clearly unable to learn as much, earn as much, obey the law as much, stay married as much, be there for their own kids as much as kids who had a father who was there for them.

As these children are growing up, they acutely miss having their Dads there. I have heard from single mothers that their kids cry and ask where their Daddy is, and that they cannot sleep at night for missing a Daddy when their friends have one. How a father can inflict this kind of pain on a child is unfathomable to me and except in very odd circumstances, unpardonable. (For vengeful mothers to deprive their children of their Daddy's company is likewise unforgivable.)

There are no wars now involving America. No legions of American men are going across the seas and prairies to fight for our freedom. The true heroes of our generation have only to do something that is in fact a true pleasure and joy: be there with Mom for their kids, openly and enthusiastically endorse Mom in front of the kids, and create a loving, complete parental environment for the kids. It's not complete with only one parent present.

10. Being a Daddy is priority number one. When you are old and facing oblivion in a nursing home or a hospital or on a golf course in winter, you are not going to wish you had spent more time at the office or making a sales call or watching a show. You will wish you had spent more time with your family. When the kids are grown up, they will not wish they had spent less time with you. In fact, when was the last time you heard a child say he wished he had spent less time with his father? Or known him less well? Or been less close with him?

Now is the time to make sure that bitter loss is not yours—or your children's. Right now, if you decide that your kids—and their Mom, because it's a package—come before your sales quota or your poker-playing schedule or your overtime to make partner, you will find that all of the other pieces of Daddyhood fall into place—teaching and learning, patience, looking for the good and praising it—because when you have more time, you are more patient, allying yourself with your kid. When you put your kids first, you are far less alone in this world. What's far more vital, so are they.

These are extremely simple rules. The real life of Daddy and child is far more complex than any rules can comprehend. But if you start with these rules as your guide, you *might* make more right decisions than wrong ones. If you truly put your kids first, you have made the rightest decision of your life.

Printed in the United States
By Bookmasters